SIGILS

Illustrated Guide to the
Symbols of Spirit and Thought

M B JACKSON

GREEN MAGIC

Sigils © 2021 by Mark Jackson.
All rights reserved. No part of this book may
be used or reproduced in any form without written
permission of the author, except in the case of
quotations in articles and reviews.

Green Magic
53 Brooks Road
Street
Somerset
BA16 0PP
England
www.greenmagicpublishing.com

ISBN 9781916014077

GREEN MAGIC

CONTENTS

Sigils	5
Sigil Craft	10
Binding	14
Number Ciphers	18
Aiq Bkr Cipher	20
Olympic Sigils	22
Golden Dawn Rosy Cross Cipher	24
Word and Statement Sigils	28
Spirit Sigils	33
Spirit Signatures	38
Spirits of the Elementary Spheres	40
Planetary Spirits	42
Planetary Glyphs	44
Planetary Signs	47
Planetary Characters	46
Planetary Kamea	48
Planetary Angels	57
Olympic Spirits	58

Sigils

Sigils are symbols designed for a specific magical purpose. They are symbolic icons that are condensed representations of more complex ideas or information. It was from astrology that the word sigil became acknowledged as an occult device with great power.

Traditionally, a sigil is a line diagram symbolizing the unpronounceable name of a spirit, a form of pictorial signature of a spirit. To know the name of a spirit gives the magician the ability to command the spirit. They are a part of the ritual of ceremonial magic used for the conjuration of angels, demons and other spirits. In more modern times, the sigil has been reinvented as a Monogram of Thought, a graphic symbol created with the sole purpose of fulfilling the magicians desired outcome, a personal desire or set of desires.

The term sigil is derived from the Latin words sigilla, sigillum and signum and in terms of magic it is generally understood to mean sign, seal, signature or little picture. Sigils are also called by different names like seal and pentacle. A seal is a sigil placed in a circle, it gives the conjuror the ability to capture the spirit and command it. A pentacle is a type of talisman drawn on floors, walls and doors, used in magic evocation for protection.

All religious symbols count as sigils and they date back to prehistory when humans first used images to infer intent - magic will - making it possible for the creator of the sigil to receive something or make something change in the Universe, themselves, in other people or to summon and control outside entities. They were part of our ancestors pictorial language in an age of symbolic literacy.

In the ancient and classic worlds of the pre-Christian era, the term 'magic' referred to arcane or esoteric knowledge. If someone had the knowledge to ward off illness or misfortune or gain favour with the gods by whatever means, they were considered to be a form of magician.

The ability to produce magic sigils to ward off evil, counteract the devil and offer protection from sorcerers and witches continued unabated into the early Judeo-Christian tradition. The Cross being the upmost symbol of protection. One difference between the priest and the sorcerer was that one employed magic for religious purposes whilst the other used it for their own ends.

The concept of the sigil became established during the Late Medieval and Renaissance period 1350-1700. During this time, magicians used sigils to call upon angels, demons and other spirits.

Each spirit had its own sigil representing its 'essence', a sort of signature or spiritual autograph. These are the high magic sigils associated with black magic. Magicians created and studied these symbols, publishing lists of them in magical training books called grimoires.

By the beginning of the 20th century, science and rationale had played a monumental role in the re-realizing of magic practise. Self-professed adepts such as Aleistair Crowley and Austin Osman Spare, rejected the traditions of Renaissance magic, taking the sigil out of ritual and employing them in their personal quests of mystical exploration as Monograms of Thought.

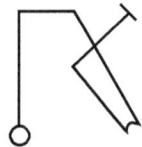

Sigil of Gabriel

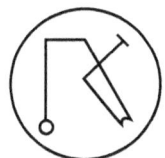

Seal of Gabriel

Pentacle of Gabriel

Thought Sigil for Gabriel

Sigil
Craft

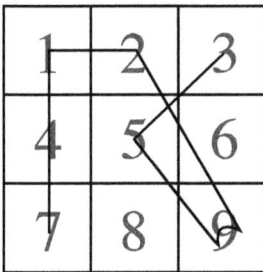

Sigil Craft

Sigils are symbolic icons, condensed representations of more complex ideas or information, designed for a specific magical purpose. Over the centuries, many different magicians have developed many different methods of creating sigils.

Traditionally, a sigil is a line diagram representing either the unpronounceable name of a spirit, or a thought symbol representing the accomplishment of a desired end, such as writing down a result in a symbolic form and then burning it to ensure its success.

Sigils are created using various techniques such as binding and number ciphers. Those sigils drawn in a continuous line are considered the most powerful. Alternatively, a sigil may have an abstract, semi-abstract or pictorial form.

Sigils have many potential uses, spiritual protection is a common one, especially when used during demonic conjuration. Sigils may appear in any medium, physical or virtual, or only in the mind. Visual symbols are the most popular form.

For magic purposes, sigils are written or engraved on to various materials including paper, wood, stone and metal, to make charms, amulets and talismans, which are burnt, kept close to the body or placed in strategic points on buildings or in the environment for protection.

Binding

Binding is the ancient technique of graphically combining key letters to form a sigil whose power is derived from the magic art of binding. It originates from the practise of using binding spells to 'bind' people up to different outcomes in sporting events, business and personal affairs related to love and even revenge.

In ancient Greece and Rome, bind spells had known formulas and named individual parties, like gods and people and connected them to actions and results.

In the modern world, Bind Runes are the most common form of this technique, although alchemical glyphs can also be bound together to form syllabic spellings for forming cryptographs and ciphers. Word and Statement Sigils also use the binding technique in the arrangement of letters to form sigils of intent.

The signs of the Zodiac, the Planets and those for the four Elements can be bound together to form symbols sometimes referred to as Elemental Sigils. Such sigils were created to represent the names of angels and, with their corresponding symbols and spirits, incorporated into the design of seals, pentacles, amulets and talismans.

SIGIL CRAFT

Linear - Stacked

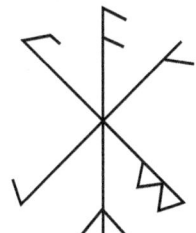

Same Stave Rune   Radial or Stave
Bind Runes

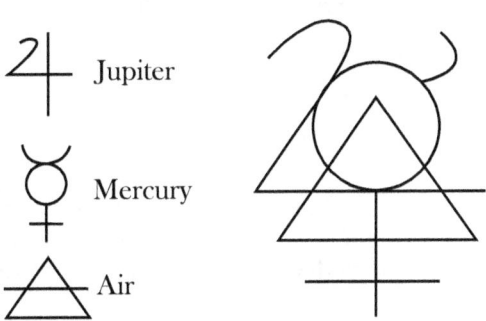

Elemental Sigil

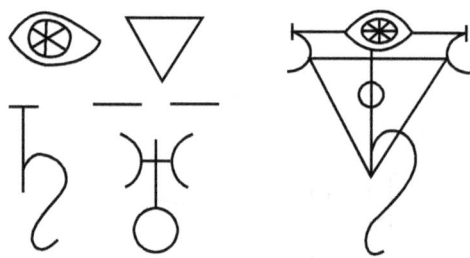

Hermetic Sigil

Seal of Aral

Center
Zodiac Fire Signs - Sagittarius, Leo, Aries
Bottom
Michael - Archangel of Fire and the South
Outer
Aral - Ruling Angel of Fire and the North

Sigil 741

Lamen

A Lamen is a term used to describe a personal seal expressing a higher or magical identity. Sigil 741 is a very specific individual application concerning spiritual families, in this case, those who consider 741 to be a dominant number in their lives. The number 741 contains three digits so the sigil is constructed from three archetypical design elements.

The number 1 relates to the Infinite One represented by the infinity sign, also expressing unity and oneness, the creative energy called God. The number 4 relates to the four directions or hermetically speaking, as above, so below. The X created in the centre of the two signs represents Amen. Lastly, 7 refers to the first seven of the thirty two paths of wisdom on the Tree of Life. From 1 or Kether, the Final Understanding or the Great Spiritual Work of Magic, to 7 or Netzach, victory or success of endeavour.

Number Ciphers

The classic and most common method of creating spirit sigils is to use the numerology associated with kamea or magic squares.

This practise stems from the technique of Isosephy invented by the Greek scholar Pythagoras, circa 600 BCE. In which each letter of the alphabet is assigned to the numbers 1 - 9. Giving the letters of a word a numerical order which can be traced out on a magic square.

The location of the numbers within the square are connected in sequence by a line to form an abstract figure that becomes the spirit's sigil or occult signature. The beginning of the sigil should be denoted by an open circle, the end denoted by a closed circle or a line. The most potent of these sigils are the ones that can be drawn in a single line without taking the pen off the paper.

Sigils formed using this method are most popularly associated with black magic and the conjuration of demons. Such sigils were published in magical training books called grimoires, most prominently during the Medieval and Renaissance era's.

3 x 3 is the most common magic square but there are many diferent kamea used to generate specific spirit sigils such as those of the planets and sephirotic angels.

SIGIL CRAFT

```
1 2 3 4 5 6 7 8 9
A B C D E F G H I
J K L M N O P Q R
S T U V W X Y Z &
```

```
G A B R I E L
7 1 2 9 9 5 3
```

Letter / Number Values

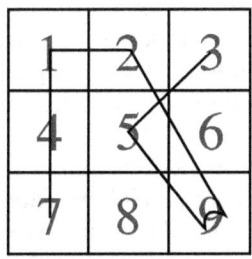

Number Cipher

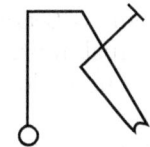

Sigil of Gabriel

Sigil of Gabriel on 3 x 3 Kamea

19

Aiq Bkr Cipher

This cipher for the English alphabet is based on the cabalistic Aiq Bkr Cipher for Hebrew. It is the original box cipher for the alphabet and was one of several similar systems described by Agrippa. It was used by the Rosicrucians, most famously in Rosalyn Chapel and the Freemasons developed several variants including the Royal Arch, Nug Soth and Blue Lodge Ciphers.

In the English version, the letters of the alphabet are arranged in a 3 x 3 grid. Each square of the grid contains three letters, written across and down, from left to right, the Ampersand is used to equal the number of letters in the Hebrew Aiq Bkr sequence.

The cipher works by taking the English spelling of the name to be ciphered and locating each letter on the grid. The letter is denoted by its position within the cell and the position of the cell within the grid.

Cells in the left and right columns and those in the top and bottom rows are marked by open right angled lines that represent their position within the square. The middle cell is shown as a square. The position of a letter in a cell is marked by a dot placed inside the right angled line showing its position. When the cipher is written, the script looks like a simple graphic design.

SIGIL CRAFT

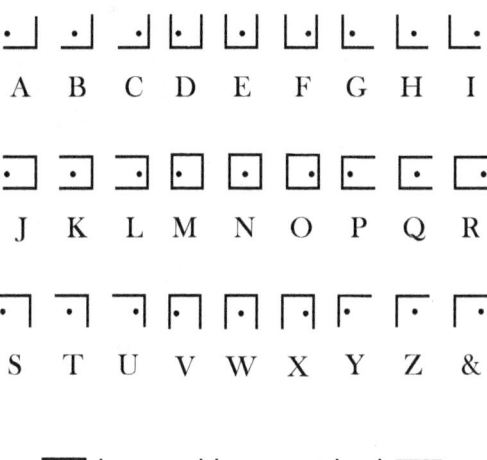

Olympic Sigils

Olympic Sigils are thought to date from before 3,000 BC, derived from central European Neolithic petrographs representing the planetary deities. It seems that their use was continued by Bronze Age blacksmiths as alchemical symbols.

Although no one is quite sure of their origin, Olympic Sigils represent the names of seven, sometimes fourteen spirits mentioned in several renaissance and post-renaissance books of ritual and ceremonial magic.

Henrich Cornelius Agrippa described how the Aiq Bkr characters can be combined to form Olympic Sigils to encode the names of angels. Although Agrippa showed several such systems, the method shown is based on one provided by Barrett in The Magus.

First, encode the name or word using the Aiq Bkr Cipher and condense its form. Next, replace the dots with vertical lines topped by triangles to further encode the sigil. To encode it further, draw a connecting line joining those letters that stand on the same line in the Aiq Bkr Cipher.

SIGIL CRAFT

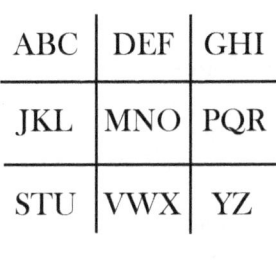

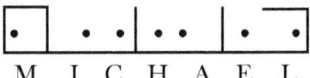

Olympic Sigil for Michael

Golden Dawn Rosy Cross Cipher

Based on the Double Star of the Sepher Yetzirah, the Rosy Cross Cipher was created by the Golden Dawn to provide a simpler and more beautiful method of constructing sigils, employing two versions to create sigils for spirits with Hebrew names.

Some of the petals on the Roman Cipher have more than one letter inside them, because the Hebrew alphabet has fewer letters than the Latin alphabet. Names of spirits spelt in English will not produce the correct sigil on either cipher.

To create a sigil on the Rosy Cross, draw a circle around the first letter of the entities name. Then draw a connecting line from letter to letter in spelling order until the last letter, when a short terminal stroke is added. The circle and terminal stroke mark the beginning and end of the sigil.

If two letters appear on the same line, a loop is added to indicate the letters. A double hump is used if a name has a double letter or two of its letters are represented on the same petal.

Once the sigil has been devised, it may be mirrored or rotated. It is frequently used for drawing sigils in the air with a magical weapon during ritual, but it may be used in the construction of any generalized sigil. There is also a version for the Enochian alphabet.

SIGIL CRAFT

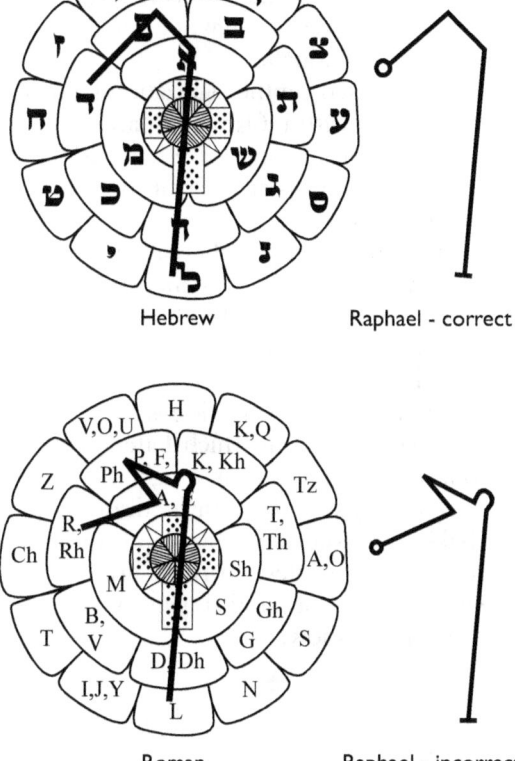

Sigil of Raphael on the Rosy Cross Cipher

Word and Statement Sigils

Word and Statement Sigils are modern forms of sigil. Modern sigils are an intention that is condensed into a single glyph, referred to as Monograms of Thought.

They are based on the sigilization techniques developed by Austin Osman Spare that have become the cornerstone of Chaos Magick, a popular form of Western occultism in the first half of the 21st century.

The common method of creating a statement sigil is to write down the intention, remove all vowels and repeat letters, then break the letters down into simple forms and arrange the letter shapes artistically.

This method of sigil creation is reminiscent of the 'binding' method in which letters are artistically bound together to form a sigil.

To activate a sigil, they maybe drawn in pastry and baked, carved into firewood or candles before burning, painted on rocks and buried or set out as decoration, and drawn in steam on a mirror or in the shower.

Word Sigils

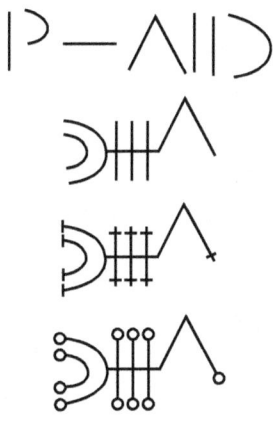

PAID

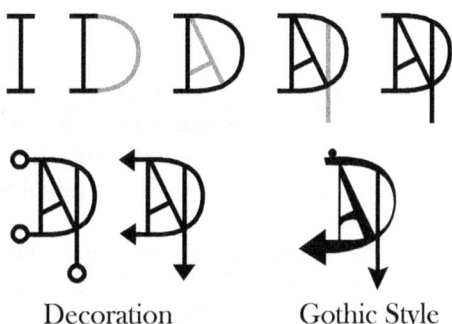

Decoration   Gothic Style
'rough hewn'

Goetic Style Word Sigil
Remove the vowels from the word sigil. Bind the remaining consonants artistically. Mark the beginning with an open circle and the terminal with a closed circle.

Mirror the sigil and bind the glyph of Mercury (Thoth/Hermes) to it. Redraw the sigil using a calligraphy pen and include other forms of symbolism to increase its magical power.

Statement of Intent Sigils

THISMYWOEALNPK
This is my wish to see a tall woman in pink shoes

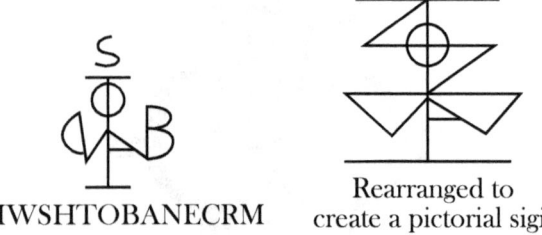

IWSHTOBANECRM Rearranged to create a pictorial sigil

I wish to obtain the Necronomicon

This is my Wish

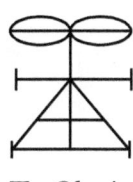
To Obtain

The Strength of a Tiger

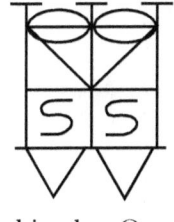
Combined as One Sigil

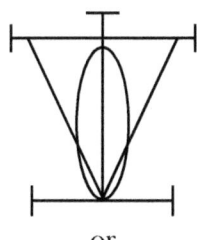
or

Spirit Sigils

Spirit Sigils

The traditional form of sigil represents the name of a spirit and in ceremonial magic there are different types of spirit for the conjurer to call upon. These entities can be classified into groups depending on their status and invoked for different reasons due to the nature of the spirit. They include planetary spirits, elementary spirits, Olympic spirits, sephirotic spirits, archangels, angels, demons and others.

The invocation of spirits using ceremonial magic was the focus of much occult practise during the High Medieval and Renaissance periods, 1350 - 1700.

Magicians recorded their practises in magical training books called grimoires, illustrated with the symbols, sigils, seals and pentacles used for the conjuration of spirits.

At this time, magic was not only a popular subject of literary works and plays, but also a very real entity in the cultural and intellectual world. European magic was academically divided in to two. Low Magic - the charms and talismans of folk magic, and High Magic - a studious mixture of Hermetism, Neoplatonism, Arabic mysticism and Jewish cabala. High Magic was more sophisticated and revered as a science to be studied. It had structure with authoritative ceremonies and detailed instructions, passed from scholar to scholar through books.

There were two types of learned magic, natural and demonic. The purpose of natural magic was to explain the occult phenomena of healing herbs and magnets. Natural magic focused on the sorcery that produced results and not so much on the rituals. Learned magic included the writing of spirits names using sigils for the ceremonial conjuration of angelic and demonic spirits.

Spirit sigils were a subject of much interest to European magicians and the Christian Church, as the magic of this period saw a peak in Necromancy; communication with spirits, both living and dead. It was the time of the Spanish Inquisition and the witch trials, when sorcerers performed magic rituals for satanic purposes.

This is mainly a falsehood as the all powerful Roman Church forbade such practises and the majority of magicians and witches would have considered themselves to be fundamentally Christian. Christianity drew on the beneficent divine power of God, archangels and angels, all other rites drew on the necessary evil force of demons who were the Fallen Angels. Magicians by the very performance of their arts, entered into pacts with demons and so became agents of the devil.

Influential grimoires included the Psuedo-monarchia Deamonum, the Occulta Philosphica and the Greater and Lesser Keys of Solomon. Following the invention of printing in 1445, published copies of magical texts were carried from mainland Europe to Scandinavia and the New World, influencing the design of the Icelandic rune staves called Galdrastafir and the Voodoo Veves of Haiti.

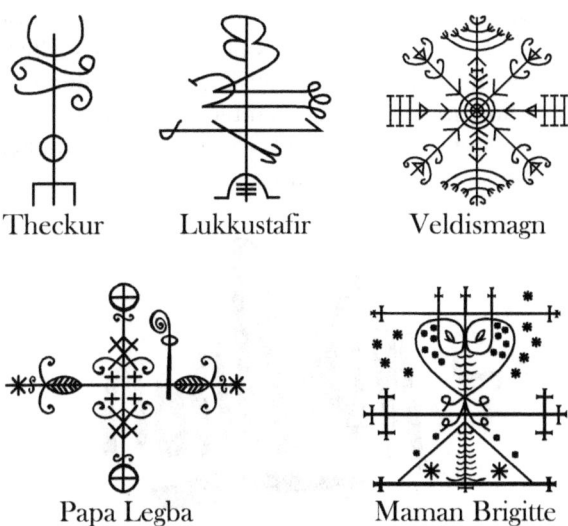

Icelandic Galdrastafir and Voodoo Veves

Spirit Signatures

Using sigils to control spirits is the primary reason sigils have existed for thousands of years. But the power of the sigil lies in the fact that an image can represent so many different concepts or desires.

A spirit signature is the actual name of a spirit written by a spirit, mainly a demon. This often occurs through the process of automatic writing or skrying.

Spirits often use obscure alphabets or letter forms and mirror their names or sign them upside down to further disguise them. Often it's not possible to read them, although they are usually a series of separate or connected forms written out in a line, in a way that resembles writing.

By contrast, spirit sigils can be more compact and resemble little pictures

Signature of the Demon Leviathan

SPIRIT SIGILS

Sigil of the Angel Belvaspata

Opening of the Mind

Love

Opening of the Heart

Praise

Opening of the Body

Gratitude

Belvaspata Healing Sigils

Spirits of the Elementary Spheres

Spirits of this type are realitively easy to contact if a magician has an understanding of the magical elements they represent.

These inteligences are very specialized, and unlike planetary spirits who often posses many areas of knowledge, each element usually has only one area of expertise in which it is proficient.

In cabala, the spirits of the spheres belong to the the Archangel Sandalphon and the sefira of Malkuth.

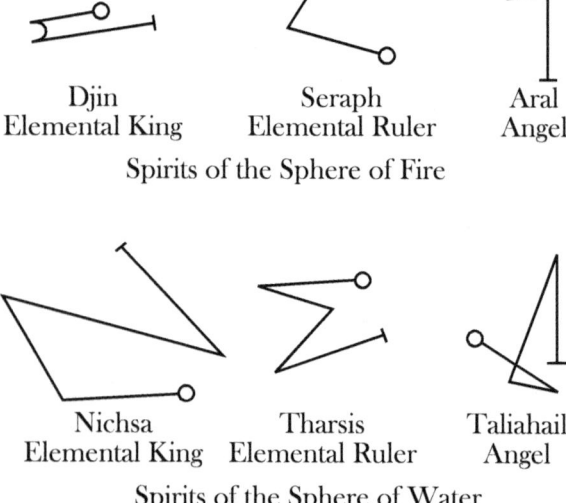

Djin
Elemental King

Seraph
Elemental Ruler

Aral
Angel

Spirits of the Sphere of Fire

Nichsa
Elemental King

Tharsis
Elemental Ruler

Taliahail
Angel

Spirits of the Sphere of Water

SPIRIT SIGILS

  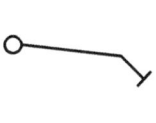

Paralda　　　　Ariel　　　　Chassan
Elemental King　Elemental Ruler　Angel

Spirits of the Sphere of Air

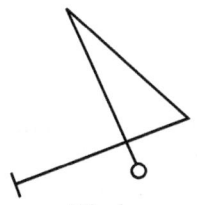  

Ghob　　　　Kerub　　　　Phorlach
Elemental King　Elemental Ruler　Angel

Spirits of the Sphere of Earth

Planetary Spirits

Planetary Spirits are some of the easiest entities to work with and may be conjured using various sets of magic symbols. They are very powerful and can help the magician in a number of related tasks simultaneously.

The term Planetary Spirits is generally applied to classes of celestial being in charge of planets or globes. They are the equivalent to the non-anthromorphical concept of archangels in Christian theology. The number of these spirits is seven, they are emanations from the Absolute and are the agents used by the Absolute to effect all changes in the Universe.

There are many levels of Planetary Spirits. The highest Planetary Spirit ruling over any globe being the Personal God of that planet. Planetary Spirits as planetary regents are concerned with natural evolution as they fashion cosmic matter.

In Western occultism, each planet has traditionally possessed a hierarchy of spirits, ethereal souls responsible for the baleful and beneficial influences of the individual planet.

Spirits associated with the planets include the Gods and Goddesses who gave their name to the planets, archangels, orders of angels, olympic spirits, planetary characters, planetary intelligences, metals, stones, minerals and plants. Their attributes closely correspond to specific sephiroth on the Tree of Life.

Planetary characters can come as sets of divine letters containing both the good and the bad spirits of the planet. There are many versions of these signs with many magicians producing their own individual variants and recording them in grimoires. In general, they are a mixture of Enochian, Alchemical and Astrological signs.

Each planet is also attributed a kamea or magic square with its own seal and spirit intelligences with their own sigils. Each of these spirits represent the magical and astrological aspects of a planet and these forces can be used to aid the magician. For example, a spirit from the Venus sphere would be helpful if a magician needed advice in matters concerning love and friendship, while a Mars intelligence would aid the magician in gaining courage and willpower.

The kamea is employed for making sigils, seals, calculating planetary hours for making and consecrating amulets and talismans.

Planetary Glyphs

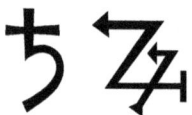
Saturn - Lead

Jupiter - Tin

Mars - Iron

Sun - Gold

Venus - Copper

Mercury - Mercury

Moon - Silver

SPIRIT SIGILS

Planetary Signs

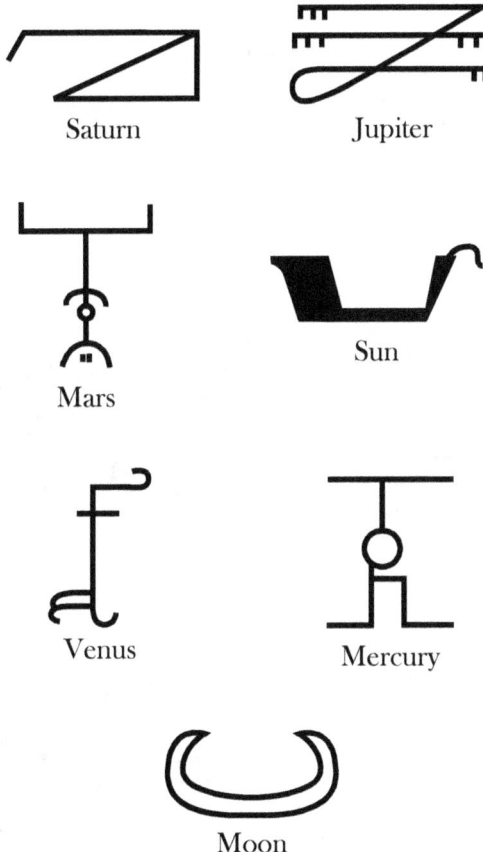

Saturn

Jupiter

Mars

Sun

Venus

Mercury

Moon

Planetary Characters

Saturn

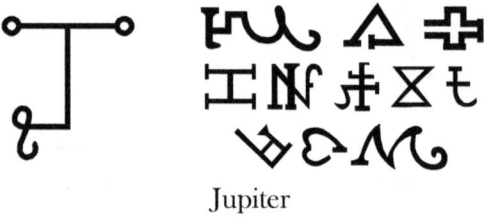

Jupiter

Mars

SPIRIT SIGILS

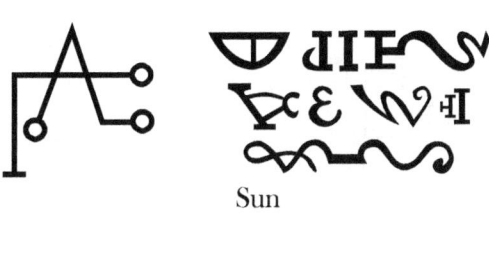

Sun

Venus

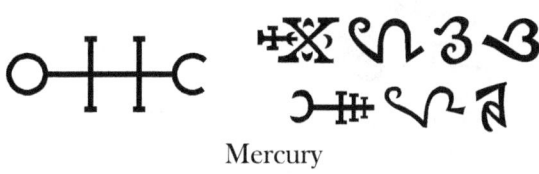

Mercury

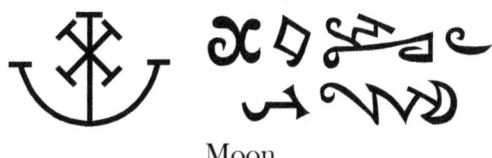

Moon

Planetary Angels

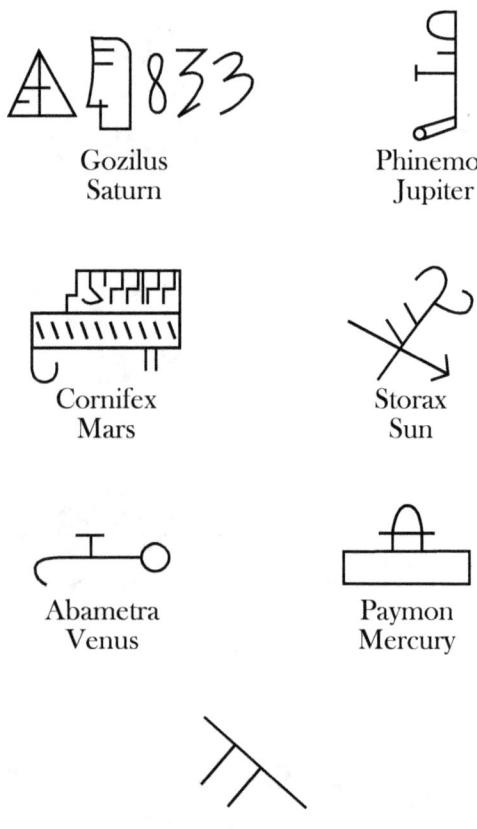

Gozilus
Saturn

Phinemon
Jupiter

Cornifex
Mars

Storax
Sun

Abametra
Venus

Paymon
Mercury

Carmelyon
Moon

Planetary Kamea

In Western occultism, there are certain kamea, magic tables or squares distributed to the seven planets. Being rightly formed, they are endowed with many virtues of heaven, representing the divine order of the celestial numbers, impressed upon them by the idea of the divine mind. The planetary kamea were published in the 16th century by Cornelius Agrippa in Da Philisophica Occultism and are a lot older.

Each kamea represents a matrix of planetary energy made up of three key numbers. The first is the planetary number. The second is the square of the planetary number, or the planetary number multiplied by itself. The third is the sum of the square or all the incremental numbers starting at one that it takes to fill the boxes in the square added together and divided by the planetary number.

Each kamea has a seal which is a geometric diagram designed so as to touch upon all the numbers of the square. The seal is used in talismanic magic to represent the entire pattern of the kamea and to act as a witness or governor for them. Unfortunately not all the seals follow the convention of overlapping every number in a kamea. Twelve numbers are missed in the seal of Venus, three are missed from Mars and some poor interpretations of the seal of the Moon don't include all the numbers.

The seal is the epitome or synthesis of the kamea and is used to block a planet's energy. By placing the seal of the planet over its kamea, it eliminates the retrograde or negative influences of the planet. The seal was used only for magical purposes, especially in the preparations of amulets and talismans.

Apart from the planetary seal, there are two planetary sigils connected to each kamea. They are called the intelligence and the spirit and are derived from key numbers of the square using techniques of gematria. Each intelligence and spirit sigil is considered an analogical glyph of the associated name, number, force, etc.

Planetary intelligences are one of the seven divine beings associated with each of the seven traditional planets of astrology. They are the part of the planet that corresponds to the mental plane of abstract thought. They are invoked in occultism to control the blind forces of the planetary spirits, specifically in the creation of amulets and talismans.

SPIRIT SIGILS

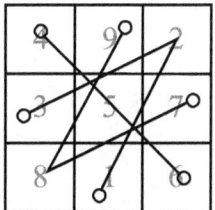

Kanea of Saturn
3 x 3 magic constant 15
total (3 x 15) 45

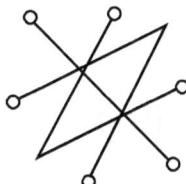

Seal of Saturn

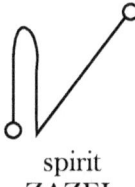

spirit
ZAZEL

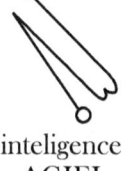

inteligence
AGIEL

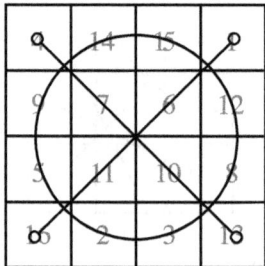

Kamea of Jupiter
4 x 4 magic constant 34
total (4 x 34) 136

Seal of Jupiter

spirit
HISMAEL

inteligence
YOPHIEL

SPIRIT SIGILS

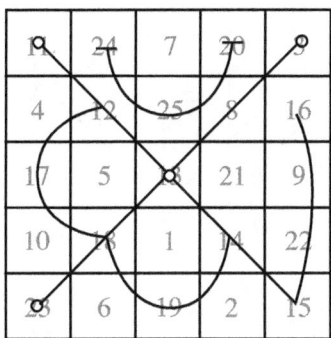

Kamea of Mars
5 x 5 magic constant 65
total (5 x 65) 325

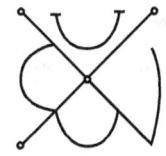

Seal of Mars

spirit
GRAPHIEL

inteligence
BARTZABEL

SIGILS

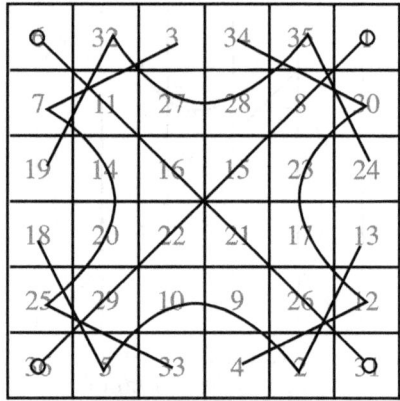

Kamea of the Sun
6 x 6 magic constant 111
total (6 x 111) 666

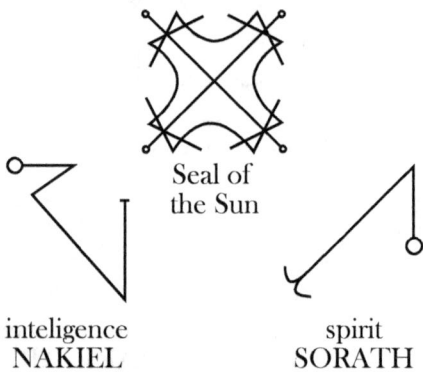

Seal of
the Sun

inteligence
NAKIEL

spirit
SORATH

SPIRIT SIGILS

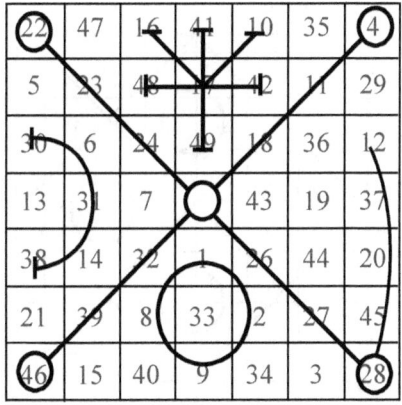

Kamea of Venus
7 x 7 magic constant 175
total (7 x 175) 1225

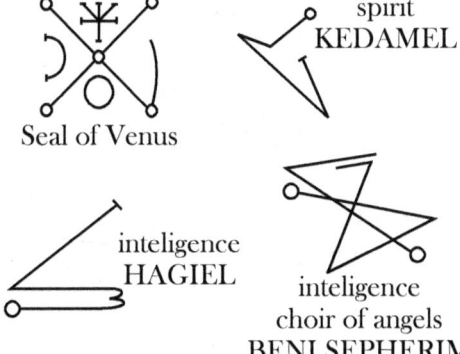

Seal of Venus

spirit
KEDAMEL

inteligence
HAGIEL

inteligence
choir of angels
BENI SEPHERIM

SIGILS

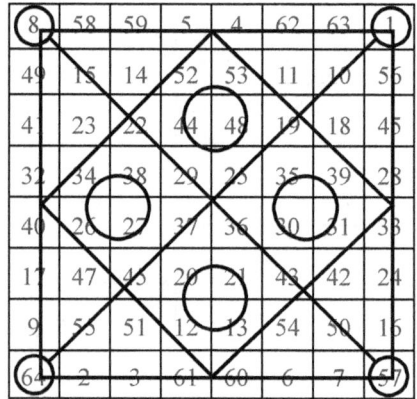

Kamea of Mercury
8 x 8 magic constant 64
total (8 x 64) 2080

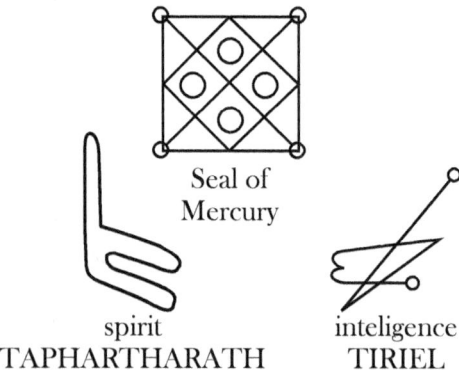

Seal of
Mercury

spirit
TAPHARTHARATH

inteligence
TIRIEL

SPIRIT SIGILS

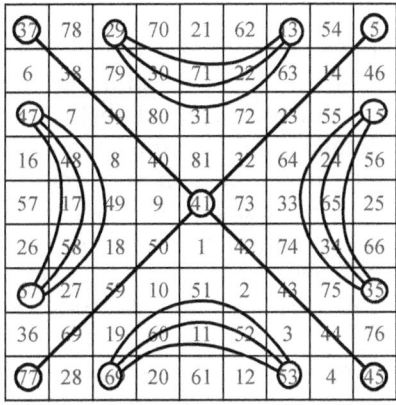

Seal of the Moon
Kameas 9x9 magic constant 369
total (9x369) 3321

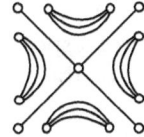

Seal of the Moon

spirit CHASHMODAI

spirit of the spirits
of the Moon

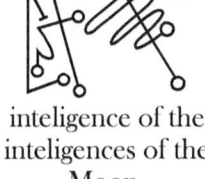

inteligence of the
inteligences of the
Moon

Olympic Spirits

A Medieval grimoire, the Arbatel of Magic, introduced these entities as the Olympic spirits, "which do inhabit the firmament, and in the stars of the firmament and the office of these spirits is to declare destinies, and to administer fatal charms, so for forth as God pleaseth to permit."

In this magic system, the Universe is divided into 196 provinces with each of the seven Olympic spirits ruling a set number of provinces.

The energies they rule correspond to the seven magical planets, and therefore these beings are very similiar to other planetary inteligences.

Some differences between the two do exist, and in many ways the Olympic entities are more useful than most planetary ones.

The grimoire called The Black Venus by Dr. John Dee illustrates three sets of sigils - Olympic, Black Venus and Ameth - that correspond to the archangels ruling the planets, not the planetary gods themselves.

These seven Olympic, Black Venus and Ameth spirits are not to be confused with the seven archangels.

They are often invoked in conjunction with the archangels and magical seals often associated one of the spirits with one of the archangels.

The Black Venus sigils were collected by Dee on his travels through Europe. They are similar in construction to Olympic sigils and both are beleived to be derived from the same archaic source.

They are thought to date from before 3,000 BC, derived from central European Neolithic petrographs representing the planetary deities. It seems that their use was continued by Bronze Age blacksmiths as alchemical symbols.

Although no one is quite sure of their origin, Olympic sigils represent the names of seven, sometimes fourteen spirits mentioned in several Renaissance and Post-Renaissance books of ritual and ceremonial magic, such as the Arbate de Magic Vererium, the Secret Grimoire of Turiel and the Complete Book of Magic Science.

The Black Venus manuscript fuses the High Magic of the Renaissance magicians with earlier practises of amalgamated goddess traditions and the absorption of these traditions into mystical Christian and Jewish sects.

The Black Venus sigils are thought to be a part of the 'underground' Dark Goddess tradition of the Cathars and Rosicrucians.

Olympic Spirts and their Sigils

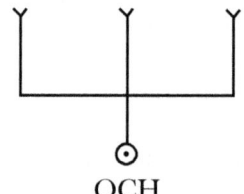

OCH
Michael, Sunday, Sun

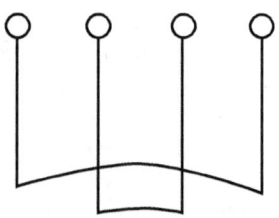

PHULL
Gabriel, Monday, Moon

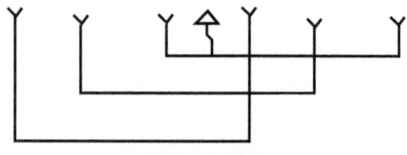

PHALEG
Camael, Tuesday, Mars

SPIRIT SIGILS

OPHIEL
Raphael, Wednesday, Mercury

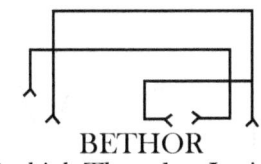

BETHOR
Sackiel, Thursday, Jupiter

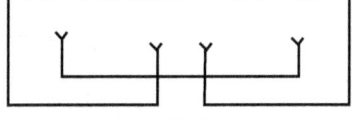

HAGITH
Anael, Friday, Venus

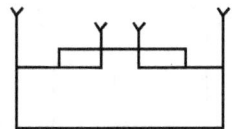

ARATRON
Cassiel, Saturday, Saturn

Black Venus Spirts and their Sigils

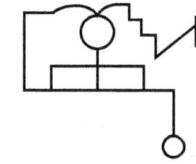

MEPHGAZUB
Michael, Sunday, Sun

MOGARIP
Gabriel, Monday, Moon

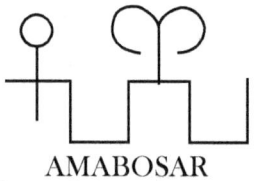

AMABOSAR
Camael, Tuesday, Mars

SPIRIT SIGILS

FALKAROIH
Raphael, Wednesday, Mercury

ALKYZUB
Sackiel, Thursday, Jupiter

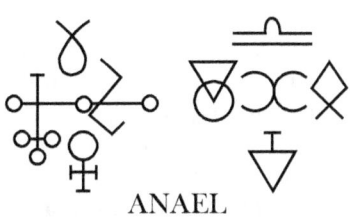

ANAEL
Anael, Friday, Venus

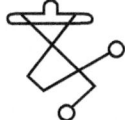

BELZAZEL
Cassiel, Saturday, Saturn

Enochian Spirits

Enochian spirits originate from a system of ceremonial magic based on the invocation and commanding of various spirits that control or govern the various sectors of the Universe.

Beginning in 1581, Enochian magic, its knowledge, language and script were all allegedly transmitted by Angels to the Renaissance occultists, Edward Kelly a psychic medium and Dr. John Dee, court astrologer to Elizabeth 1. Over a period of seven years, Dee and Kelly accumulated a great quantity of work, including an entire language with its own unique alphabet and syntax.

This secret Angelic language became known as Enochian, because it was last revealed to the Hebrew patriarch Enoch by the Angel Ave. Kelly, as the receiver of the language, wrote his texts in Enochian, the resulting book is called Liber Loagath, 'Book of the Speech from God'. It consisted of 49 great letter tables or squares made up of 49 x 49 letters. Each table has a front and a backside making 98, 49 x 49 tables in all.

A year later, Kelly received a second set of texts. These have English translations, providing the basis for Enochian vocabulary. The texts comprise 48 poetic verses, which Dee calls 'Claves Angelicea' or Angelic Keys. The overt purpose of the keys was to establish ritual communication with the spirits of the 30 Aethyrs or Airs who rule over the tutilitary spirits of the nations of the Earth.

There are actually 49 calls, the first is too sacred and mysterious to be voiced, the second conjures spirits, the next 16 conjure elements, fire, water, air, earth, the 19th opens the gates to any of the 30 Aethyrs, evoked by the remaining 30 calls.

Each of the 30 Aethyrs is populated by 3 Governors except for one that has 4, totaling 91. Each of the 91 Governors has a sigil, a symmetrical character which can be traced onto the Great Table. The Governors names are formed by the letters these sigils connect, revealing the order of the world according to the ideal plan of God.

The Great Table is formed by four tablets, each ruled over by an element, they are the chief overseers or Watchtowers of the points of the compass. When properly aligned, they form the Great Table.

Dee and Kelly never performed Enochian magic because the angels told them not to use it. It was rediscovered in the 1880s by the Golden Dawn and Anton Le Vey adapted it to his Satanic System in the 1960s.

Fire / South
O HEOO AA A TAN

Earth / North
THA HAA OTH E

Water / West
THA HE BY O A AT NUN

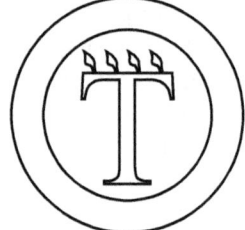
Air / East
TA HAO EL OG

The Four Watchtowers
The four cardinal points or four quaters, North, South, East and West. They are also associated with the four elements, Air, Fire, Water, Earth.

They are used to call upon the aid of angels ruling over the four directions and invoked during ritual of casting a magic circle.

SPIRIT SIGILS

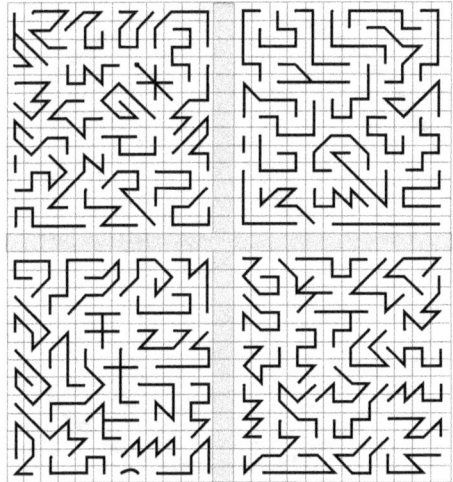

Great Table of Earth

The Enochian map of the Universe is depicted as a square made up of the four elemental tablets or Watchtowers. This square is called the Great Table of Earth and is divided into quadrants called Watchtowers by the Black Cross.

Each of the Watchtowers and hence the Great Table show the sigils of the Governors, symmetrical characters which can be traced onto the Great Table's 91 palaces, regions of the astral realm connected to each of the earthly territories controlled by the Governors.

Ameth Sigil and Seals

Enochian seals are powerful pentacles used to bind demons, protect an area from angels interference and conceal humans from every angel in creation. The seals are mainly derived from the Sigils of Ameth, as angels instructed Dee and Kelly to recreate it, inscribed with names of God and various angels. The names of the Ameth angels are found on the outer ring of the sigil. They are synonymous with the Olympic and Black Venus spirits of the 7 planets, connecting them to the 7 Archangels and the 7 week days.

SPIRIT SIGILS

AAOTH - Michael
Sunday, Sun

GALAS - Gabriel
Monday, Moon

INNON - Camael
Tuesday, Mars

THAOTH - Raphael
Wednesday, Mercury

HORLWYN - Sackiel
Thursday, Jupiter

GALETHOG - Anael
Friday, Venus

GETHOG - Cassiel
Saturday, Saturn

Archangels

In the angel hierarchies of the Christian tradition there are three spheres of angels containing three orders or choirs of angels. Those closest to God appear in the first sphere in the order of Seraphim, Cherubim and Thrones. The second sphere contains Dominations, Virtues and Powers. The third sphere contains Principalities, Archangels and Angels. Archangels are the chief angels or first in rank and act as messengers or envoys.

The earliest reference to a system of seven archangels is in the Book of Enoch, their names being Gabriel, Michael, Raphael, Uriel, Raqael, Remiel and Saraqael.

As well as their Hebrew names, there are also Christian and Islamic variants, leading to a divergence of correspondence among them.

Various occult systems associate each archangel with one of the seven planets and as such they also correspond to the days of the week and both are associated with certain deities, angels, spirits, colours of the rainbow, metals and zodiac signs.

The 'luminary' sigils of the 'angels of the days of the week' were published by Francis Barrett in The Magus in 1801 but their origins are unknown.

SPIRIT SIGILS

Pentacle of Michael

Sigil of Michael
"Who is like God"
The Warrior

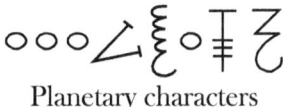

Planetary characters

Archangel Michael - Sunday

Moon — Cancer

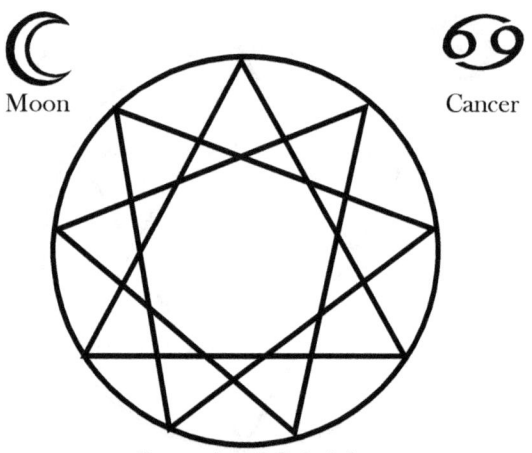

Pentacle of Gabriel

Sigil Of Gabriel
"Strength of God"
The Messenger, Strength and Mercy

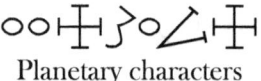

Planetary characters

Archangel Gabriel - Monday

SPIRIT SIGILS

Pentacle of Samuel

Sigil of Samuel
"One Who Sees God"
Bearing Joy, Concernment

Planetary characters

Archangel Samuel (Camael) - Tuesday

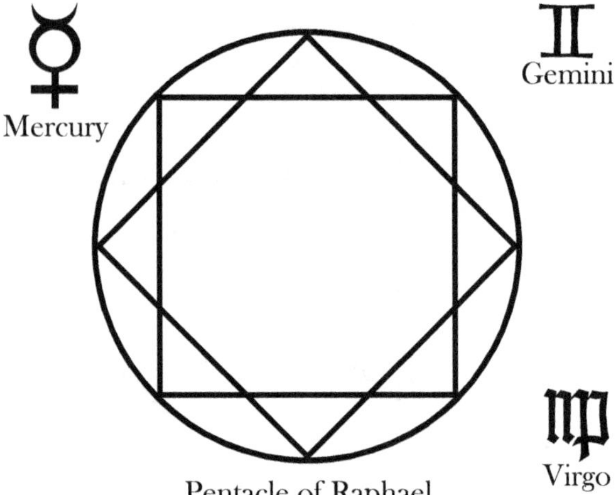

SIGILS

☿
Mercury

♊
Gemini

♍
Virgo

Pentacle of Raphael

Sigil of Raphael
"God Heals" Healer,
Teacher, Guide

Planetary characters

Archangel Raphael - Wednesday

SPIRIT SIGILS

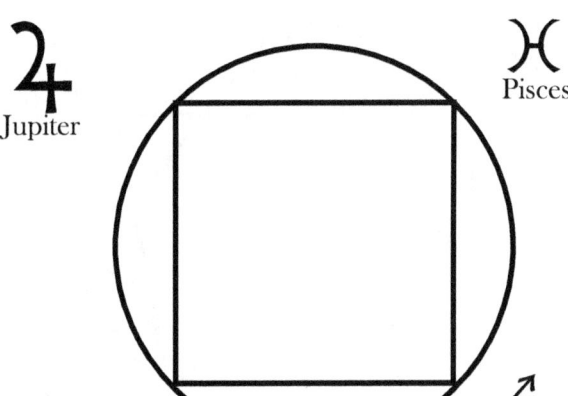

Pentacle of Zadikiel

Sigil of Zadikiel
"Cowering of God"
Wealth, Charity

Planetary characters

Archangel Zadikiel / Sachiel - Thursday

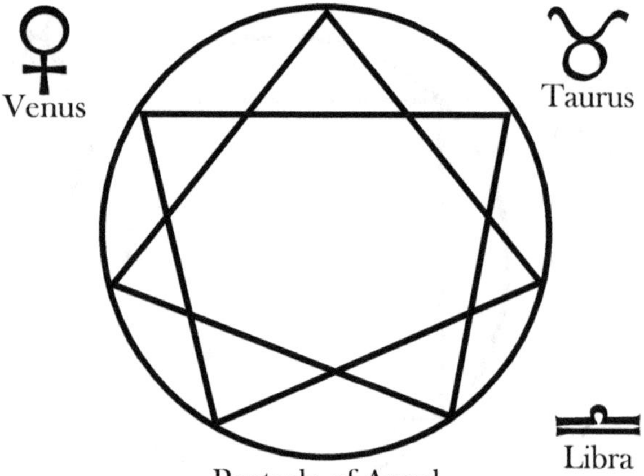

SIGILS

Venus

Taurus

Pentacle of Anael

Libra

Sigil of Anael
"Joy of God"
Sexuality, Creation

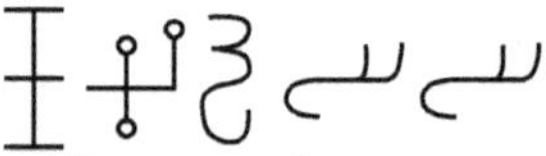

Planetary characters

Archangel Anael (Anniel) - Friday

SPIRIT SIGILS

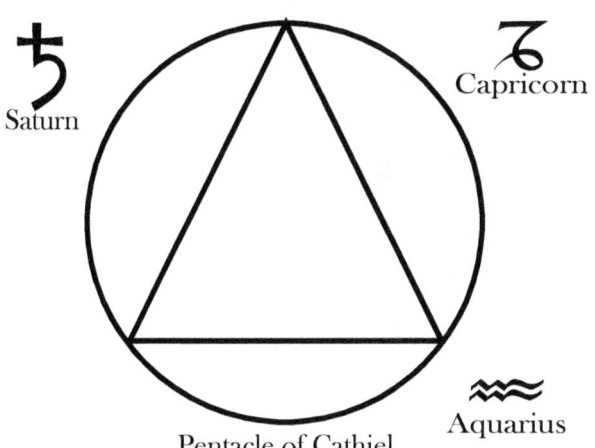

Pentacle of Cathiel

Sigil of Cathiel
"Speed of God"
Solitude, Patience, Temperance

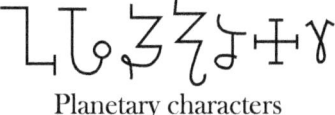

Planetary characters

Archangel Cathiel (Cassiel) - Saturday

Celestial Sigils of the Archangels

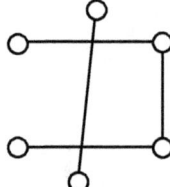

Michael

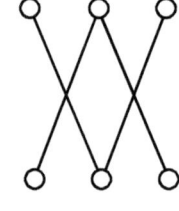

Gabriel

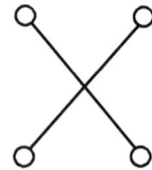

Raphael

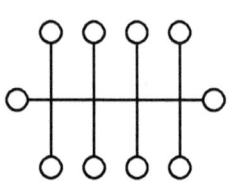

Anael
Samuel

SPIRIT SIGILS

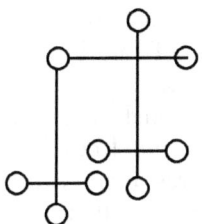

Camael / Tzadkiel

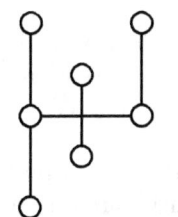

Cassiel / Kaphziel

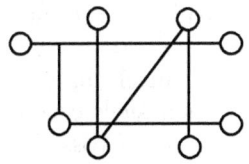

Sachiel / Zadkiel / Anathiel

Sephirotic Angels

According to cabala as described by the Golden Dawn, the Tree of Life illustrates how God the Creator, expressed his creative energy throughout the Universe, through angels and on to human beings. Each of the trees branches are called sephiroth, spheres that symbolize a particular type of creative force that a different archangel oversees. There are ten sephirotic archangels, each corresponding to one of the sephiroth.

Cabalistic angels are forces that send information and sensation between mankind and the Tetragramaton or YHWH. Because of this, it is reasoned that they should not be worshipped, prayed to, nor invoked. When they appear, they are seen only from the viewpoint of the recipient, which will be anthropomorphic.

Sephirotic angels are known for their work for justice. The most important of the them is Metatron, the second most powerful being in the Universe after God himself. Sandalphon is considered the 'brother' of Metatron, he is the leader of the Ishim those angels closest to humans.

The sephirotic angels have no set or traditional form and their sigils can be derived using the Golden Dawn Rosy Cross Cipher.

SPIRIT SIGILS

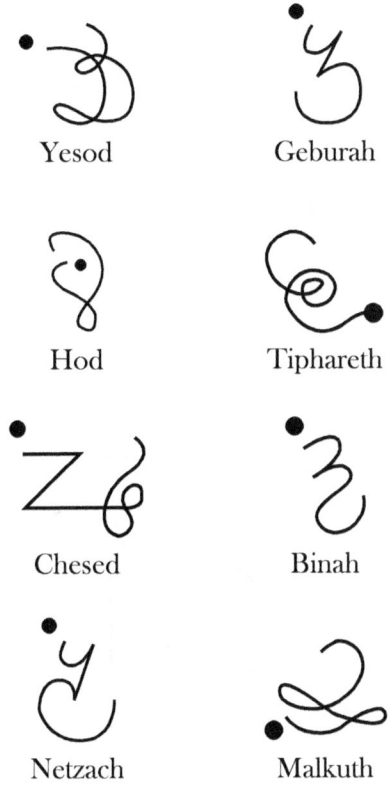

Aurum Solis Presigiliums for Some of the Angels of the Sephirotic Tree

Sephirotic Angels

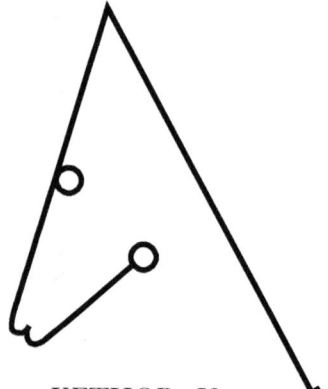

KETHOR - Uranus
Archangel Metatron

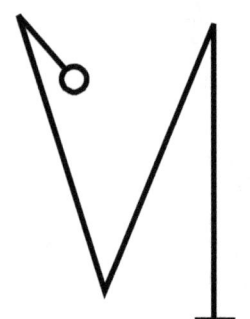

CHOCKMAH - Neptune
Archangel Raziel

SPIRIT SIGILS

BINAH - Saturn
Archangel Tzaphqiel

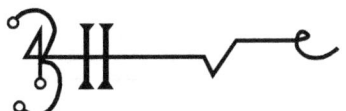

CHESED - Jupiter
Archangel Tradqiel

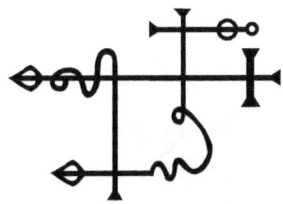

GEBURAH - Mars
Archangel Kamael

SIGILS

TIPHERET - Sun
Archangel Raphael

NETZACH - Venus
Archangel Haniel

HOD - Mercury
Archangel Michael

SPIRIT SIGILS

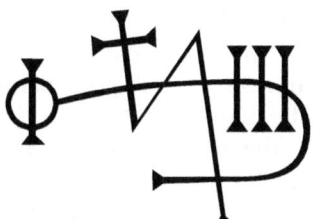

YESOD - Moon
Archangel Gabriel

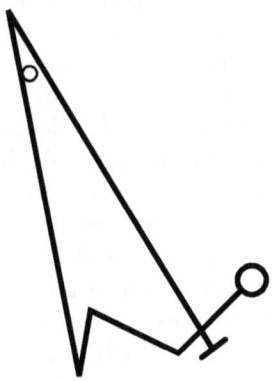

MALKUTH - Earth
Archangel Sandalphon

72 Angels of the Shemhamphorash

These angelic spirits originate from the cabalistic Shemhamphorash or 72 fold name of God, describing the hidden names of God. The 72 angels being the mystical name of God. Shem means Divine Name, the name is Tetragrammaton - YHWH - who is Supreme Lord of the 4 Elements or the Whole Universe.

The angels names are devised using a special arrangement of 216 consecutive letters of the 3 verses numbered 19, 20 and 21, taken from Exodus, concerning a formula used by Moses to part the Red Sea. The formula is a key to the Sefer Raziel and a key component of the Lesser Keys of Solomon. It can also grant Holy men with the power to counteract demons.

The letters of the verses are written out to form triplets by taking the first letter of verse 19 - Vau, the last letter of verse 20 - Heh, and the first letter of the 21st verse - Vau, to make the first triplet - VHV. This is repeated to create the remaining names. The result provides the three consonants to form each of the 72 holy names. The three letter names of God become the names of angels by adding either IEL or IAH (YAH) to the end of each name. Their sigils are created using the method of encoding names by means of number ciphers.

The 72 angels primarily serve God and carry out missions from God to men, but many serve directly as Guardian Councilors, Guides, Judges, Interpreters, Cooks, Comforters, Matchmakers and Grave Diggers.

In Solomonic magic, the 72 Angels of the Shamhamphorash protect the conjuror from the 72 Goetic demons they are numerically paired with. Each angel controls and counters a specific demon, typically of the same number. There is a discrepancy in the demons number system so it doesn't directly match up.

The 72 fold name was mentioned by Roger Bacon and the angels of the Shemhamphorash featured in the cosmology Johann Reuchin, influencing Agrippa and Kircher.

Rudd featured them in his magic as a balancing force against the evil spirits of the Ars Goetia or in isolation. Rudds material was later used by Blaise de Vigenoe, whose manuscripts were used by modern magicians like MacGregor Mathers in his work for the Golden Dawn.

SIGILS

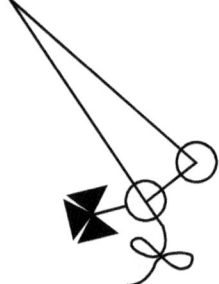

1. Vehuaiah
Subtle spirit endowed with great wisdom, enthusiastic for science and arts. Capable of undertaking the most difficult things.

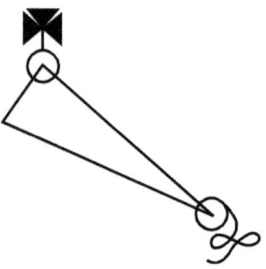

2. Jeliel
To quell popular uprisings. To obtain victory over those who attack unjustly. Sprightly spirit agreeable, courteous, passionate for sex.

3. Sitael

Against adversities. Protects against weapons and wild beasts. Loves truth, will keep his word. Will oblige those in need of his services.

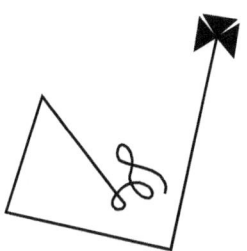

4. Elemiah

Against mental troubles and for identification of traitors. Governs voyages, sea travels, industrious, successful, keen for travel.

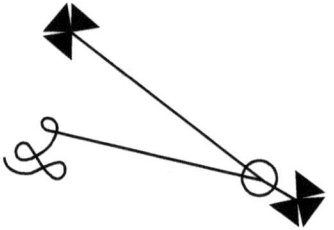

5. Mahasiah
To live in peace with everyone. Governs high science, occult, philosophy, theology, liberal arts, learns easily. Keen for honest pleasures.

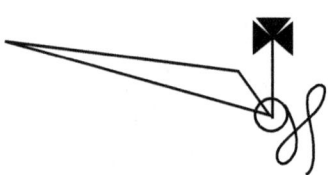

6. Lalahel
To give knowledge and cure disease. Governs love, renown, science, arts and fortune. Features include ambition.

SPIRIT SIGILS

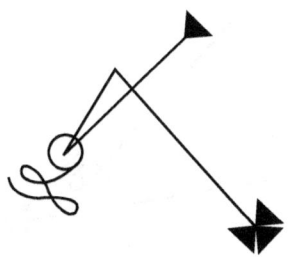

7. Achaiah

Governs patience, secrets of nature. Loves learning, proud to accomplish the most difficult tasks.

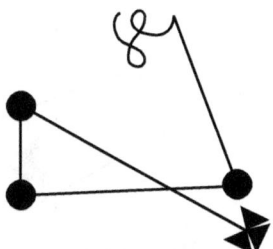

8. Camethiel

To attain the benediction of God and drive away evil spirits. Governs agricultural production. Inspires men towards God.

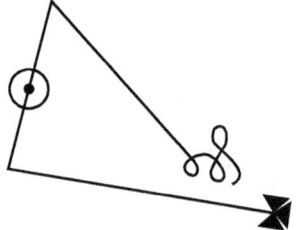

9. Haziel (Aziel)

Mercy of God, friendship and favour of the great, execution of a promise made. Governs good faith and reconciliation. Sincere in promises, will easily extend any pardon.

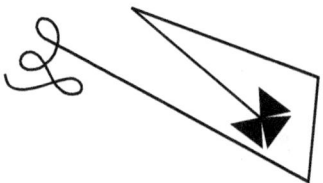

10. Aladiah

Good for those guilty of hidden crimes and fearing discovery. Governs rage and pestilence, cure of disease. Good health successful in his undertakings.

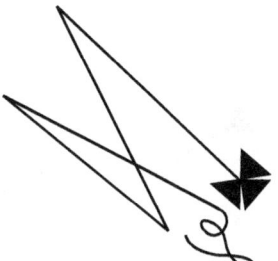

11. Lauviah

Against lightening and for the obtainment of victory. Governs renown. Great personage, learned, celebrated for personal talents.

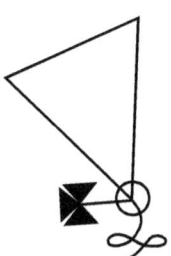

12. Hahaiah

Against adversity. Governs dreams, mysteries hidden from mortals. Gentle, witty, discreet, manners.

SIGILS

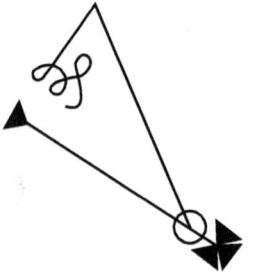

13. Iezalel
Governs knowledge and reconciliation, conjugal fidelity. Learns easily, adroit.

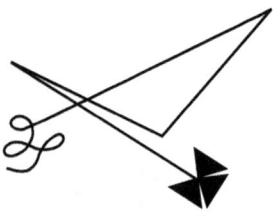

14. Mebahel
Against those who seek to usurp the fortunes of others. Governs justice, truth, liberty. Delivers the oppressed and protects prisoners. Loves jurisprudence, affinity for law courts.

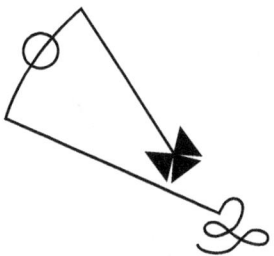

15. Hariel
Against the impious. Governs science and arts. Religious sentiments. Morally pure.

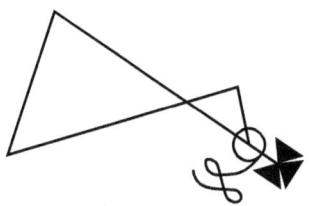

16. Hekamiah
Against traitors and for the deliverance from those who seek to oppose us. Governs crowned heads, great captains. Frank, loyal, brave character.

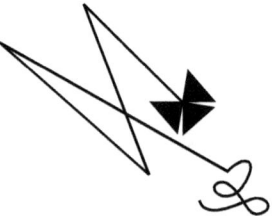

17. Lanoiah

To be invoked while fasting. Against mental anguish, sadness. Governs high science, marvellous discoveries, gives revelations in dreams. Loves music, poetry, literature and philosophy.

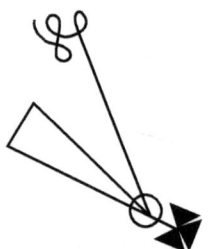

18. Caliel

To obtain prompt aid. Makes truth known in lawsuits, causes innocence to triumph. Just, honest, loves truth, judiciary.

SPIRIT SIGILS

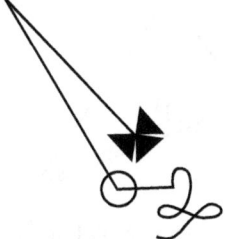

19. Leuviah
To be invoked while facing south. To obtain the grace of God. Governs memory, human intelligence. Amiable, lively, modest, bearing of adversity with resignation.

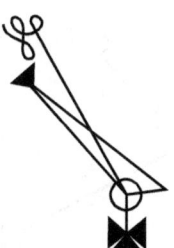

20. Pahaliah
Against enemies of religion, for the conversion of nations to Christianity. Governs religion, theology, morality, ecclesiastical vocation.

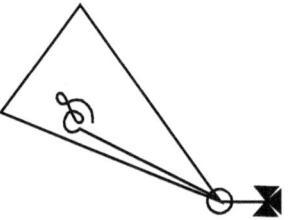

21. Nelchael

Against calumniations and spells and for the destruction of evil spirits. Governs astronomy, mathematics, geography and all abstract sciences. Loves poetry, literature, avid for study.

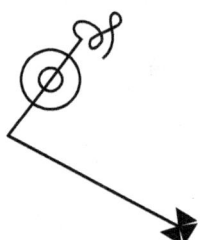

22. Yeiayel (Ieiael)

Governs fortune, renown, diplomacy, commerce. Influences on voyages, discoveries. Loves business, industrious, liberal and philanthropic.

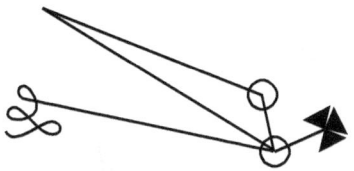

23. Melahel

Against weapons and for safety in travel. Governs water, produce of the earth and especially for plants necessary to cure disease. Courageous, accomplishes honourable actions.

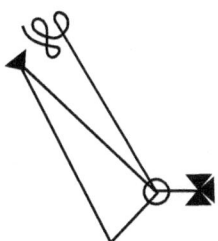

24. Hahuiah

To obtain the mercy of God. Governs exiles, fugitives, defaulters, protection against harmful criminals. Preserves from thieves and assassins. Loves truth, the exact sciences, sincere in word and deed.

SIGILS

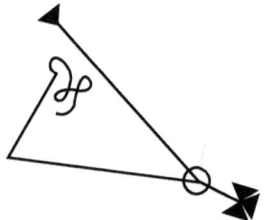

25. Nith - Halah

For the acquisition of wisdom and the discovery of the truth of hidden mysteries. Governs occult sciences, gives revelation in dreams, particularly to those born on the day over which he presides. Influences those who produce the magic of the sages.

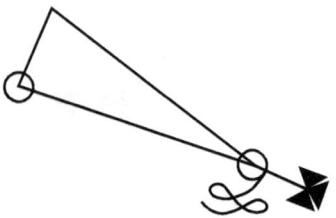

26. Haaiah

For the winning of a lawsuit. Protects those who search after the truth. Influences politics, diplomats, secret expeditions and agents.

SPIRIT SIGILS

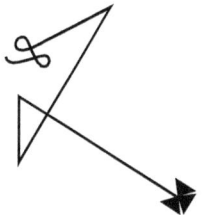

27. Yerathel (Jerathiel)
To confound wrongdoers and liars and for the deliverance from ones enemies. Governs propagation of light, civilization, love, peace, justice, science, arts, special affinity for literature.

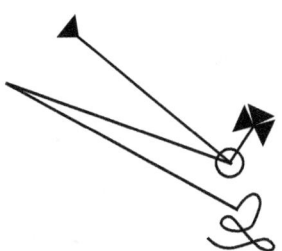

28. Seheiah
Against infirmities and thunder, protects against fire, the ruin of buildings, falls and illness. Governs health, simplicity. Has much judgement.

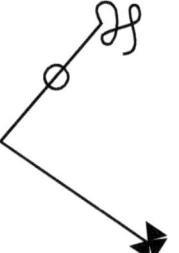

29. Reyiel (Reiel)

Against the impious and enemies of religion, for deliverance from all enemies both visible and invisible. Virtue and zeal for the propagation of truth, will do his upmost to destroy impiety.

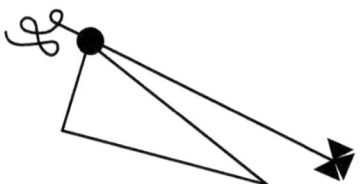

30. Ornael (Omael)

Against sorrow, despair and for the acquisition of patience. Governs animal kingdom, watches over the generation of beings, chemists, doctors, surgeons. Affinity for anatomy and medicine.

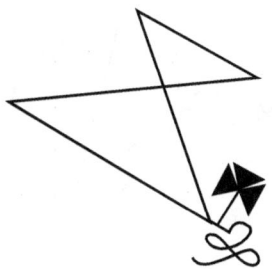

31. Lecabel

Fortune, acquisition of knowledge. Governs vegetation and agriculture. Loves astronomy, mathematics and geometry.

32. Vasariah

Against those who attack us in court. Governs justice. Good memory, articulate.

SIGILS

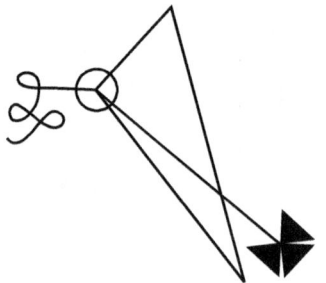

33. Yehuyah (Iehuiah)
For the identification of traitors.

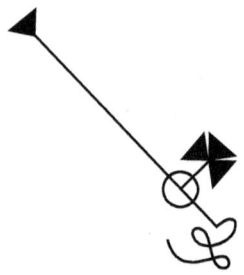

34. Lehahaiah
Against anger. Known for his talents and acts, the confidence and fervour of his prayers.

35. Chevakiah

To regain the favour of those one has offended. Governs testaments, successions and all private financial agreements, Loves to live in peace with everyone. Loves rewarding the loyalty of those in his service.

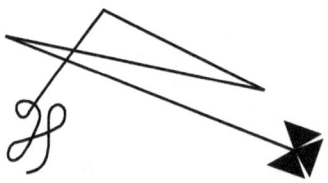

36. Menadel

To retain ones employment and preserve ones means of livelihood. Against calamity and the deliverance of prisoners.

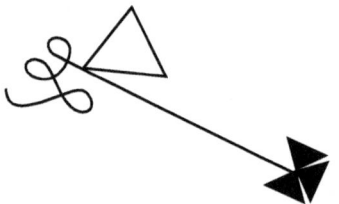

37. Aniel
To obtain victory and stop the siege of a city. Governs sciences and arts. Reveals the secrets of nature and inspires philosophers and sages. Distinguished savant.

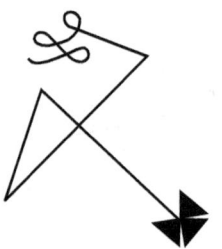

38. Haamiah
For the acquisition of all treasures of heaven and earth. Against fraud, weapons, wild beasts and infernal spirits. Governs all that is related to God.

SPIRIT SIGILS

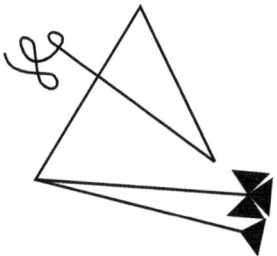

39. Rehael
For the healing of the sick. Governs health and longevity. Influences paternal and filial affection.

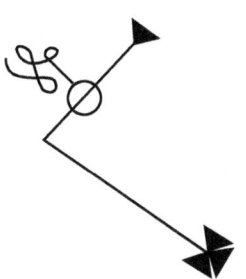

40. Yeiazel (Ieiazel)
For the deliverance of prisoners, for consolation, for deliverance from ones enemies. Governs printing and books, men of letters and artists.

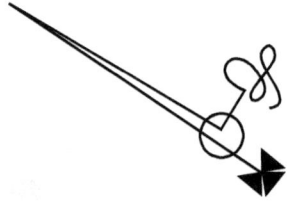

41. Hahamel
Against the impious, slanderers. Governs Christianity, greatness of soul energy, consecrated to the service of God.

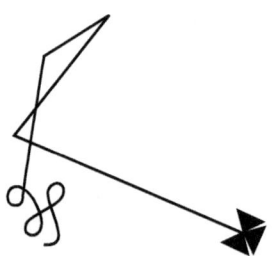

42. Mikael
For safety in travel. For the discovery of conspiracies. Concerned with political affairs, diplomatic.

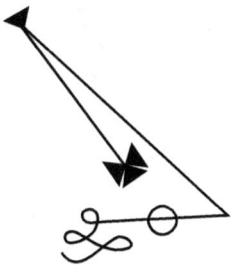

43. Veuliah
Fortune. Destruction of the enemy and delivers from bondage. Loves glory and the military.

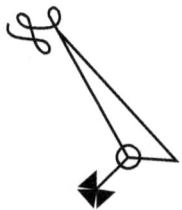

44. Yelaiah (Ielaliah)
Success of a useful undertaking. Protection against magistrates, trials. Protects against armies, gives victory. Fond of travel and learning. All his undertakings are crowned with success. Distinguished for multiple capabilities and courage.

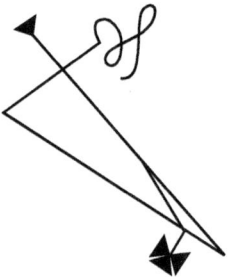

45. Sealiah
To confound the wicked and the bravery to exhalt the humiliated and the fallen. Governs vegetation. Loves learning, much aptitude.

46. Ariel
To procure revelations. To thank God for the good he sends us. Discovers hidden treasures, reveals the greatest secrets of nature, causes the object of ones desire. Strong, subtle mind, new and sublime thoughts.

SPIRIT SIGILS

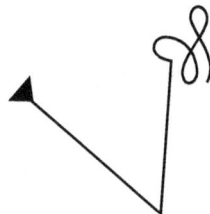

47. Asaliah
For the praising of God and the growing towards him when he enlightens us. Governs justice, makes the truth known in legal proceedings. Agreeable character, distinguished of secret knowledge.

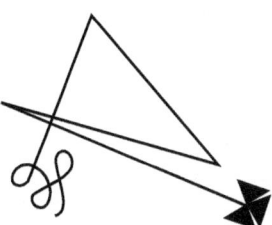

48. Mihael (Michael)
For the preservation of peace and the union of man and wife. Protects those who address themselves to him. Gives premonitions and secret inspirations. Governs generation of beings. Loves walks and pleasure in general.

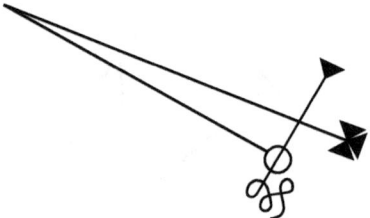

49. Vehuel

Sorrow. For the exultation of oneself and the benediction of God. Sensitive and generous soul, Literature, jurisprudence, diplomacy.

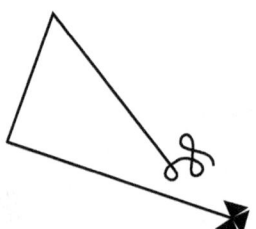

50. Harael - Daniel

To obtain the mercy of God and consolation. Governs justice, lawyers, solicitors. Furnishes consciousness to those who hesitate. Industrious and active in business. Loves literature and is distinguished for eloquence.

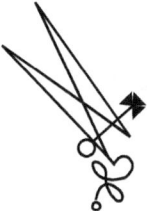

51. Hahasiah

For the elevation of the soul and the discovery of the mysteries of wisdom. Governs chemistry and physics. Reveals the secret of the philosophers stone and universal medicine. Loves abstract science. Devoted to the discourse of the principles of animals, plants and minerals. Distinguished in medicine.

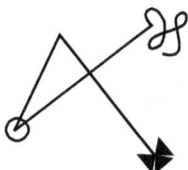

52. Imamiah

Destroys the power of enemies and humbles them. Governs voyages in general. Protects prisoners who turn to him and gives them the means to obtain their freedom. Forceful, vigorous, temperant, bears adversity with patience and courage. Fond of work.

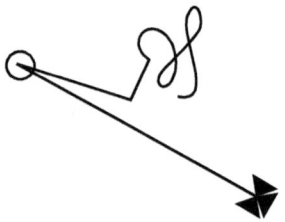

53. Nanael

Governs the high sciences. Melancholy, humour, avoids rest, meditation. Well-versed on the abstract sciences.

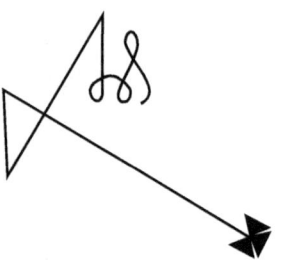

54. Nithael

To obtain the mercy of God and live long as emperor, king or prince. Renowned for eloquence, of great reputation among the learned.

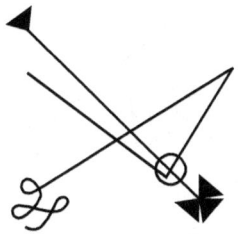

55. Mehahiah

Beneficial for obtaining consolation and compensations. Governs morality and religion. Distinguished by good deeds and piety.

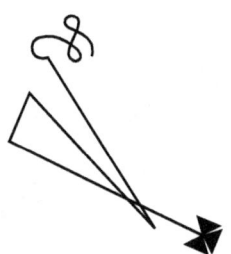

56. Poyel (Poiel)

For the fulfilment of ones request. Governs renown, fortune and philosophy. Well esteemed by everyone for his modesty and agreeable humour.

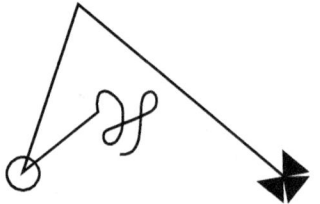

57. Nemamiah

For the general prosperity and the deliverance of prisoners. Governs great captains. Drawn to the military. Distinguished for activity and the courageous bearing of fatigue.

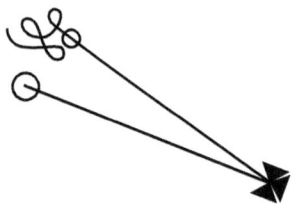

58. Yeialel (Ieialel)

Protects against sorrows and cures and heals the sick, especially afflictions of the eye. Influences iron and those in commerce. Brave. Frank, affinity for Venus.

SPIRIT SIGILS

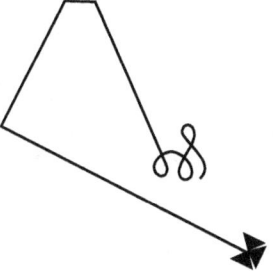

59. Harael

Against the sterility of women and to make children obedient to their parents. Governs treasure and banks. Love of learning, successful in business.

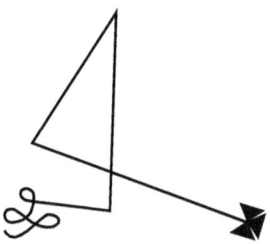

60. Mitzrael

For the cure of mental illness and deliverance from those who persecuted us. Virtuous. Longevity.

SIGILS

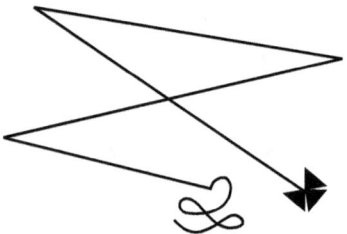

61. Umabel
To obtain the friendship of a given person. Fond of travel and honest pleasures, sensitive heart.

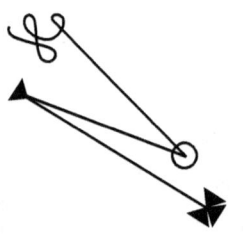

62. Iah-El (Iah-Hel)
For the acquisition of wisdom. Governs philosophy, illuminati. Loves tranquility and solitude, modest and virtuous.

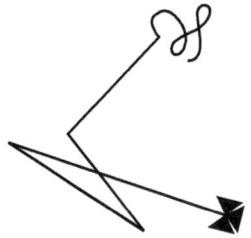

63. Ananel

For the conversion of nations to Christianity. Protects against accidents, heals the sick. Governs commerce, banking. Ingenious, industrious and active.

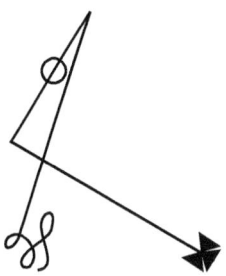

64. Mehiel

Against adversities, Protects against rabid and wild beasts. Governs savants, professors, orators and others. Distinguished in literature.

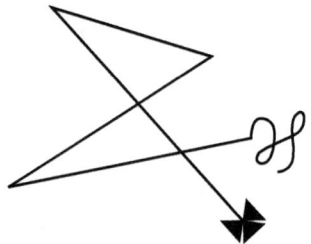

65. Damabiah
Against magic spells and for the obtainment of wisdom and the undertaking of successful ventures. Governs seas, rivers, springs, sailors. Amasses a considerable fortune.

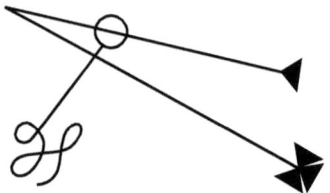

66. Manakel
For the appeasement of the anger of God and for the healing of epilepsy. Governs vegetation, aquatic animals. Influences dreams. Gentleness of character.

SPIRIT SIGILS

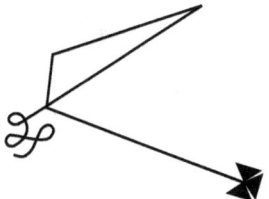

67. Eyael (Iiaiel)
To obtain consolation in adversity and for the acquisition of wisdom. Influences occult sciences. Makes the truth known to those who call on him to in their work. Enlightened requirement of the spirit of God. Distinguished in the higher sciences. Fond of solitude.

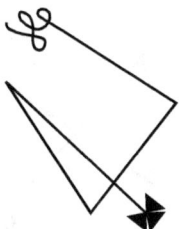

68. Mabuhiah / Chabuhiah
For the preservation of health and the healing of the sick. Governs agriculture and fecundity. Fond of the countryside, hunting, gardens and all that is related to agriculture.

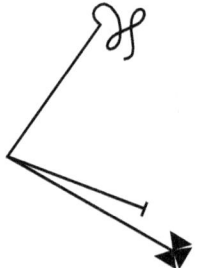

69. Rochel

To find lost or stolen objects and discover the person responsible. Distinguished in the judiciary, morals and customs of all peoples.

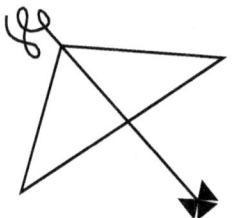

70. Jabamiah (Iabamiah)

Governs the generation of beings and phenomena of nature. Protects those who wish to progress spiritually. Distinguished by genius, one of the great lights of philosophy.

SPIRIT SIGILS

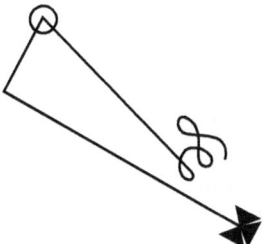

71. Haiaiel
To confound the wicked and for deliverance from those who seek to oppress us. Protects those who call upon him. Influences fire.

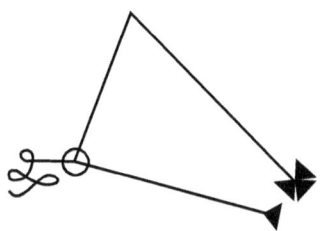

72. Muniah / Mumiah
A divine talisman. Protects in mysterious operations, brings success in all things. Governs chemistry, physics, medicine. Influences health and longevity.

Demonic Spirits

Belief in demons goes back many millennia, Zoroastrianism teaches that there are 3,333 demons, some with specific dark responsibilities such as war, starvation, sickness, etc, Some believe these concepts are received as part of the cabalistic tradition. Others perceive demons were part of healing magic used to describe medical conditions such as epilepsy and mental illnesses.

The Christian Church held that the world was pervaded with spirits and advanced the belief that demons received worship directed at pagan gods. A number of authors throughout Christian history have written about demons. Texts like the Pseudomaonarchia Daemonum and the Lesser Keys of Solomon are written with instructions on how to summon demons in the name of God.

These texts were usually more detailed, giving names, ranks and descriptions of demons, although this may vary according to each grimoire. Some of the number, names and sigils of demons featured by Agrippa and Kircher differ to those of the Lesser Keys of Solomon, although they are in essence the same spirits.

Some scholars suggest the origin of early demonology can be traced to two distinct mythologies of evil - Adamic and Enochic. The Adamic story traces the source of evil to Satan's transgression and the Fall of Man. The Enochic tradition bases its demons on the story of the Fallen Angels led by Azazel. Enochic demons are formed from the names of the Fallen Angels listed against their transgressions, taken from the Book of Enoch.

By the Renaissance, they had become a mixture of Greek, Jewish, Christian, Arabic and other traditions. The ranks given to the spirits, Marquis, Duke, Count, Knight are European in origin.

SIGILS

Very Old Sigils for Demons

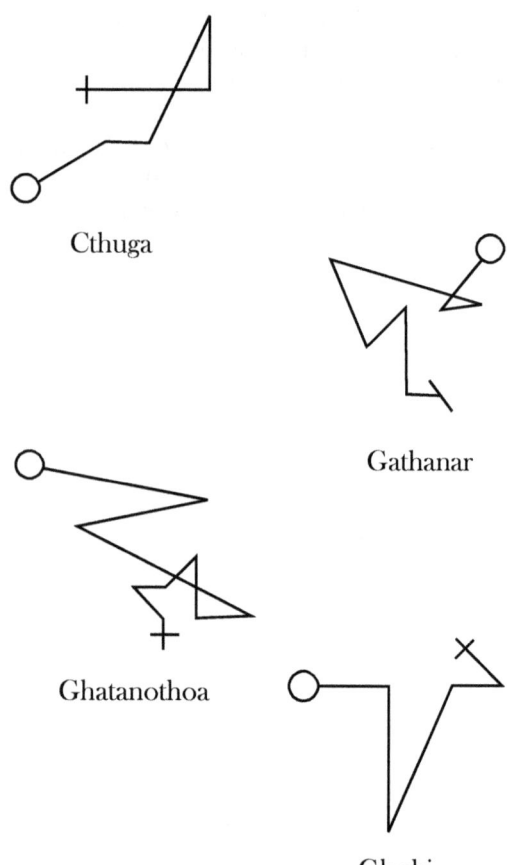

Cthuga

Gathanar

Ghatanothoa

Glaaki

SPIRIT SIGILS

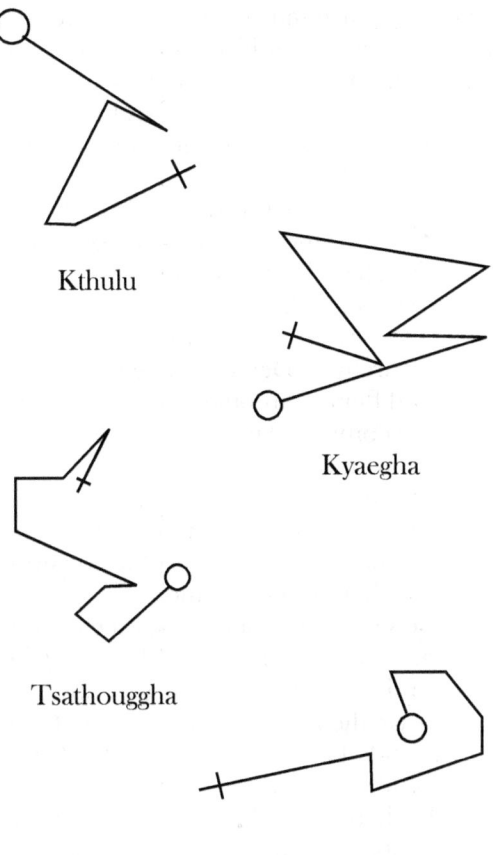

Kthulu

Kyaegha

Tsathouggha

Y'golonak

Goetic Spirits

In the modern mind, Goetic spirits are the evil spirits associated with black magic. They are the demons summoned by King Solomon who contained them in a bronze vessel marked with sigils and commanded them to build his temple.

They take their name from the Ars Goetia or Howling Arts, the first section of the 17th century grimoire called the Lesser Keys of Solomon. Originally called the Spirits of the Seals, they are also known as the 72 Princes of the Hierarchy of Hell, the Spirits of the Brazen Vessel and the False Monarchy of Demons. The Lesser Keys of Solomon differs from other goetic texts because entities are compelled into obedience, rather than asked for favours.

In Solomonic magic they are the demons numerically paired with the 72 Angels of the Shemhamphorash, who protect the conjuror and control the demons he summons.

Goetic sigils were a subject of much interest to European magicians and the Christian Church. Those spirits identified as being amongst the 72 were re-classified as demons by the Christain Church and became the subject of various grimoires like the Lesser Keys. Many devotees were shocked and dismayed at their spirits re-classification as a demon, in particular those of

Astaroth, previously the Goddess Astarte, before the Christian Church reassigned her name and gender.

Described as being commanded by the four kings of the cardinal directions, the Goetic spirits are divided into two groups for white or black magic purposes. Combined, the spirits accomplish all abominations. While some of these spirits seem a little evil at first glance, practice shows that many of them perform useful tasks, such as healing and teach a great number of useful things, such as language and sciences. They are easy to command and are far from demonic in nature.

In the 20th century, the Hermetic Order of the Golden Dawn revived Solomonic magic. The Ars Goetia portion of the Lesser Keys of Solomon was translated by MacGregor Mathers and published by Aleister Crowely in 1904 under the title of The Book of the Goetia of Solomon the King.

Black Magic Seals of the Spirits

Agares/Agreas

Provides knowledge of all tongues, brings back runaways or can prevent desertion, can cause earthquakes, and bring about the downfall of important men causing them to lose their position, public honour and respect of others.

Aim

He spreads destruction by means of fire. Also teaches cunning and shrewdness, and will answer questions of things unknown.

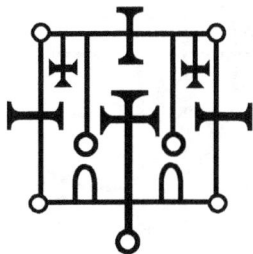

Alloces/Alocas

A warrior who may be sent to revenge yourself from secret enemies.

Andras

Very destructive, he can bring ruin to an enemy in the twinkling of an eye, causing him financial havoc and personal despair.

Andrealphus

Can transform humans into birds at will. Also teaches mathematics.

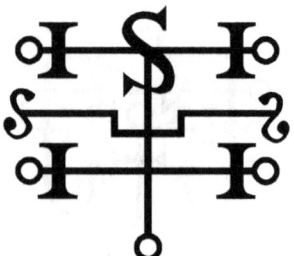

Andromalus

Knows all, recovers lost articles, finds money and reveals any secret plots of intrigues planned against the possessor.

SPIRIT SIGILS

Asmonday / Asmondai

Confers invisibility, answers any questions and enables the petitioner to know the innermost thoughts of those he meets.

Bathin

Transports from one place to another at the speed of light by supernatural means. To tell the virtues of all stones and herbs.

Bifrons / Bifrous / Bifrovs

Can move corpses magically, and coerce spirits of the dead to assist the magician or answer inquires. Is capable of enlightening one on astrology, mathematics, herbs and stones.

Camio / Caim

Will teach the tongues of all tongues so that they may be understood, and can also reveal the mysteries and secrets of the other worlds.

SPIRIT SIGILS

Crocell / Krokel

Produces great noise, confusion and indecisiveness in one's foes. Gives knowledge of geometry, art, literature and history.

Dantalion

Produces hallucinations in others if requested, influencing the minds of men against their will and without their knowledge. He can reveal the innermost thoughts and desires of others.

SIGILS

Decarbia
Knows all pertaining to plants and stones.

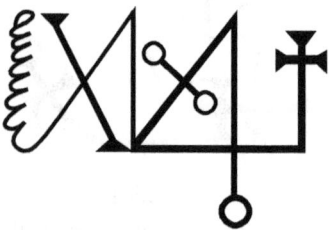

Focalor
Causes winds to blow, ships to sink and death by drowning.

Furfur

Bestows love of battle, causes thunder and lightening and can reveal the secret thoughts of others.

Glasya-Labolas

Can cause murder and death, makes men invisible. He knows all ancient wisdom and occult secrets, can teach all sciences.

SIGILS

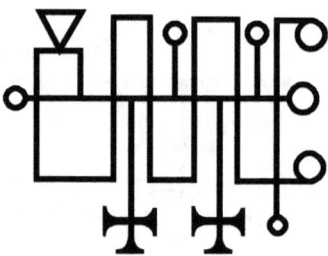

Haagenti

A powerful alchemist who can change any metal into gold and water into wine.

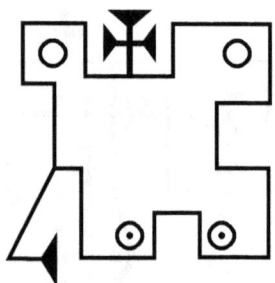

Halphas

Causes wars, punishes sinners and can make those who have wronged the magician suffer the torture of the dammed.

Haures

Protects the magician against other spirits. Knows all secrets and will bring harm to one's foes.

Leraie

Causes wounds not to heal, starts battles. He can be persuaded to break up rival's love affairs and even marriages.

Malphas/Malthus/Malthous/Malthas
It is claimed he helped Solomon build many things. Causes anything to be made by magic forces.

Murmur/Murmus/Murmux
Causes souls to appear and answer any questions the petitioner may ask. Also teaches philosophy.

Ose/Voso/Oso

Transforms the petitioner into any form he desires. Will bring delusions and insanity to others if asked and the person affected will not be aware that he has been changed.

Paimon

Confers upon the magician the power to influence and control those he wishes to subjugate. Will produce familiars to serve the possessor and bring any honour desired upon one.

Purson

Tells past and future, reads the thoughts of others and conveys the message to the possessor.

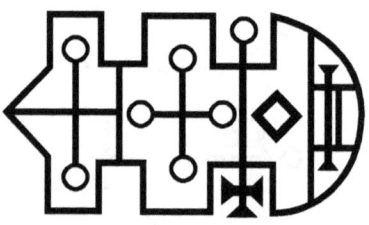

Raum

Creates love and reconciles enemies. Can also demolish a reputation, destroy property and will steal money to bring to the possessor.

SPIRIT SIGILS

Ronove

Teaches languages and humbles an enemy who does not show partiality toward the petitioner.

Sabnock

Can cause wounds not to heal, arguments to inflame and turn a small dispute into a full-scale battle. He controls military camps and protects soldiers.

Samiginia/Gamigin
Gives account of the dead souls that died in sin and teaches the liberal sciences.

Seere/Sear/Seir
Controls time to suit himself and the wishes of the sorcerers who call upon him. Can cause things to happen instantly magically.

Shax/Shaz/Shass/Shan

Can cause one to become deaf, dumb or blind. Will steal money or possessions and can lead the way to almost any hidden thing or stolen goods. Can create a familiar to assist the owner.

Sitri

The Prince of Love and Lust. Will cause any man to love a woman or any woman to desire a man. Compels women to display themselves in the nude to the one who calls them.

Valefor

In charge of occult medicine, curing all ills magically. Can make a man skilled with his hands and sharp with his brains, Can change men into animals at will.

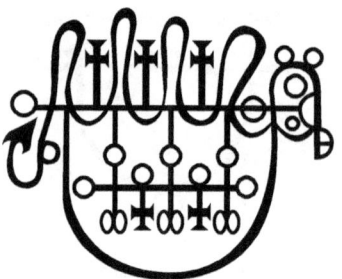

Vepar/Vephar

Controls the sea. Can cause storms, death and disaster.

Vine/Vinea

The only spirit which will tell the magician the identity of other sorcerers and witches. Knows all secrets and can destroy the enemy or defend the magician against the attacks of others.

Zagan

Can change liquids - water into wine, wine into blood. He can bring to one's mind the humour and wit in all happenings.

White Magic Seals of the Spirits

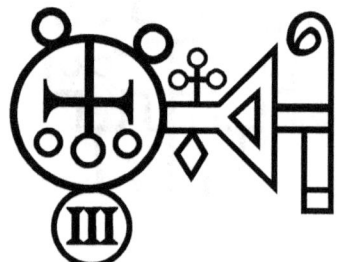

Amdusiars/Amdukias

Can have a familiar assist in any secret mission one may wish performed. Can inspire music and cause trees to be barren of fruit or even fall to the ground.

Amon

Reconciles enemies, causes love to flourish and tells what is to happen in the future.

SPIRIT SIGILS

Amy

Shows the way to hidden treasure, fortune and wealth. Can teach astrology to the practitioner who asks.

Astaroth

Teaches any scientific subject, causes one to have prophetic dreams or visions about the future and even gives insight into the unknown.

Bael

Gives the needed wisdom to assist one in making the correct decision when faced with seemingly insurmountable problems.

Balam/Balaam

Confers humour, wit and mental ability to those who ask.

SPIRIT SIGILS

Barbatos

Brings any two together in friendship, smooths out all misunderstandings and smooths hurt feelings. This spirits seal is only usable under the sign of Sagittarius.

Beleth/Bileth/Bilet

Brings the spirit of love between any two persons. A favorite of maidens awaiting a proposal.

SIGILS

Belial

Helps one get ahead on the job or to get a higher position. Brings praise and favours from others, even from ones foes.

Berith/Beale/Beal/Bofry/Bolfry

Causes men to rise to high places and receive honours. Can change any metal into gold. Answers questions about future happenings.

Botis

Gives assistance on important decisions, bolsters courage, protects one from being hurt by the hatred and envy of others and helps towards easing tensions in the home.

Buer

Cures illness and disease magically, discourages drunkenness, provides knowledge of logic and philosophy.

Bune/Bime/Bim

Helps acquire wealth, provides sophistication and wisdom, grants facility of speech and a flair with words.

Cimejes/Cimeies/Kimaris

Makes all who ask bold of heart, firm of spirit and heroic in battle. Teaches literature and finds anything that is lost.

Eligos

Grants favours in court cases and legal affairs, creates love, attracts business and financial success.

Foras

Can make one wise, witty and wealthy. Restores lost property. Teaches logic and the virtues of stones and plants.

SIGILS

Forneus

Can teach all arts, sciences and language. Can make one's enemies love him and protects him from evil doers.

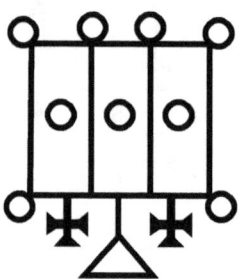

Furcas

Brings peace of mind and dispels fear and timidity. Also can teach philosophy and other sciences.

Gaap

Causes love or hate, tells the future and can make one transport instantaneously to wherever he desires.

Gremory/Gamon

Causes one to be beloved by women (and is the only spirit to appear as a woman). Knows past, present and future and will lead to hidden gold and treasure.

Gusion

Can grant position, bring honours and make those who are unliked beloved by all with whom they come into contact.

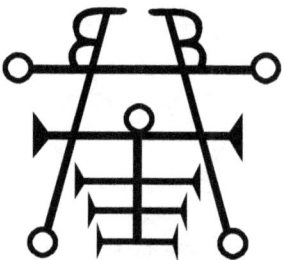

Ipos

Endows wit and courage. Helps one retain friends and make new ones. Has knowledge of the past and future.

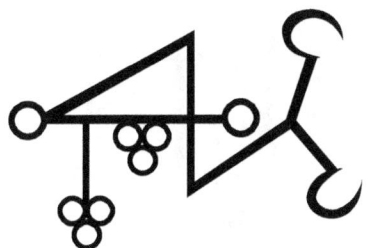

Marax/Morax

Will provide a familiar to assist the magician. Gives knowledge in the magical uses of stones and herbs, teaches astrology.

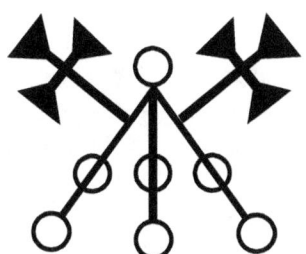

Marbass

Gives great wisdom and knowledge. Answers questions about secret, hidden or stolen things. Can cure or cause diseases.

SIGILS

Marchosias
Assists in any kind of fight, argument or battle.

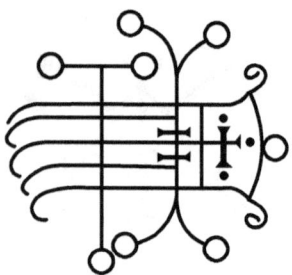

Naberius
Teaches logic, rhetoric and helps one regain lost honours, prestige or possessions.

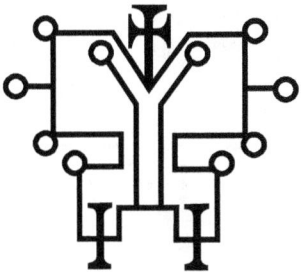

Orias/Oriax

Induces enemies to favour the petitioner. Can change men into any shape. Helps gain respect and positions of esteem.

Orobas

Answers questions and gives one the power to control and dominate others. Suppresses slander or gossip and makes one secure from the persecution of evil spirits or vindictive foes.

Phenex/Pheynix
Obeys every order. Speciality is poetry and letters.

Sallos/Saleos
Causes love between the sexes, arousing desire, stimulating one's passions and encouraging fidelity to one's mate.

SPIRIT SIGILS

Stolas/Stolos
Knows all of the stars, plants and stones.

Valac/Volac/Volak/Valu/Ualav
Tells where treasures may be found and can lead one to a good job, a sympathetic friend or a lucky number.

SIGILS

Vapula/Naphula
He can assist one in passing tests and examinations and in conversing intelligently on almost any subject.

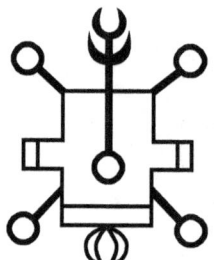

Vassago
Can tell of the past and future and find anything that has been misplaced, lost, hidden or stolen.

Vual/Voval/Uvall

Can make one beloved of women, create friendships and insure esteem. Knows all and can turn time to suit himself.

Zepar

Can make any woman love any man or compel any man to love any woman. He can also change the shape of people as desired.

Thought Sigils

Thought Sigils

From the end of the 17th century, European elites became disenchanted with magic and embraced the scientific revolution of the Enlightenment, the Age of Reason and the Baroque philosophy of Isaac Newton, Rene Descartes and others.

The invention of the optical lens for telescopes and microscopes changed astrology into astronomy and alchemy into science. Magnifying glasses and spectacles enabled intellectuals to study for greater lengths than ever before, reading well into their old age.

The influence of magic on the human mind dissipated, witchcraft laws began to be repealed, marking the beginnings of the modern world.

The legacy of Renaissance High Magic reached a peak of notoriety with Aleister Crowely and the Hermetic Order of the Golden Dawn at the end of the 19th century.

At the beginning of the 20th century, Crowley and a later contemporary, the English artist and mystic Austin Osman Spare sought to reform aspects of ceremonial magic.

Spare went on to develop his own theories of magic which became the cornerstone of Chaos Magick, the foremost system of Western occultism in the early 21st century.

Austin Osman Spare

Born in 1886, Austin Osman Spare was an English artist and occultist who developed his own unique techniques of automatic writing, automatic drawing and sigilization. His work has had a huge effect on modern western occultism, his teachings became a cornerstone of Chaos Magick.

Spare's iconoclasm and aversion to morality, as well as his sigilisation, served to distinguish his personal style of magic from others.

It focuses on one's individual universe and the influence of the magician's will on it. Consequently, it is a highly personal.

Essentialy, Spare turned the medieval practise of using sigils to evoke entities on its head, arguing that such supernatural beings were simply complexes in the unconcious and could be actively created through the process of 'sigilization'.

The big diference with Spare's method was that he dispensed with pre-existing esoterica and external beliefs, so that sigils were no longer for controlling tradtitional demons, angels and other spirits, but instead for controlling forces in the unconcious psyche of the individual operator or magician. Ultimately, he refined the use of sigils by themselves, i.e. outside of ritual.

His technique known as 'sigilisation' became the core element of Chaos Magick and from there has developed into a popular element of Western occultism.

Spare was inspired by reading Blavatsky, Agrippa and Eliphas Levi and had a brief association with Aliester Crowley, who initiated him into the Arum Argentius.

In 1913, Spare pubished the Book of Pleasure (self love) The Psychology of Ecstacy, in which he presented his own magical system involving the creation and use of sigils, trance states, sexual sorcery and a personal philosophy of pleasure, obsession and the subjective nature of reality.

The Book of Pleasure also featured his similiar automatic writing and drawing techniques used by the Surrealists. The sigils and emblems produced the letters of Spare's so-called Alphabet of Desire claiming that each letter in its pictorial aspect relates to a sex principle.

It is Spare's most influential work and remains one of the most unique magical works of the 20th century. Spare died in obscurity in 1956.

In 1975, Spare's long time friend and fellow Thelemite, Kenneth Grant, wrote the first major work on Spare's sorcery and was instrumental in bringing Spare out of the shadows into the forefront of 20th century occultism.

Spare is associated with Zos Kia Cultus. The term was coined by Kenneth Grant, who used it to refer to the system of magic developed by Spare that nvolves complex symbolism of form, sound, desire and will, deriving from sexual energy.

Key to Spare's magico-religious views were dual concepts of Zos and Kia. Spare describes Zos as the human body and mind, as a whole, which could project desires and modify the world of matter, he later adopted the term as as a psuedonym for himself.

Spare used the term Kia, pronounced 'keah' or 'keer', to refer to the universal mind or ultimate power, akin to the idea of Brahman in Hinduism or the Daoist idea of the Dao.

Although Zos Kia Cultus has had a huge effect upon on modern Western occultism, especially Chaos Magick, it was a short lived movement. It largest branch is now in the USA, known as the Monastery of the Seven Rays.

THOUGHT SIGILS

Spare's sex magic-religious sigilization

first
comative

increative or
hermaphrodite

Alphabet of Desire

An alphabet of desire is a set of symbols an individual creates that represents various magical goals, functions, intents, processes, etc.

Spare's sentient symbols and his alphabet of desire situate his mediatory magic in the realms of Tantra, or cosmological properties.

The basis of this alphabet, together with many early examples of the letters composing it, is given in Spares Book of Pleasure, where he ascribed his use of art and sex to explore the subconscious mind.

THOUGHT SIGILS

abstract creating
per as

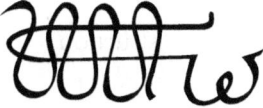

copulating the ether
masturbation
simulation

abartive
sodomy

Sex Principles

Alphabet of Desire

theory

noncoporeal
SUBJECTIVE

belief

atrophy

destruction
DEATH

release

loathing

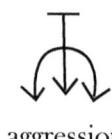
aggression
HATE

anger

aversion

fright
FEAR

terror

THOUGHT SIGILS

joy

attraction
DESIRE

greed

doubt

corporeal
OBJECTIVE

known

dissolution

lust
SEX

frustration

rapture

passion
LOVE

attachment

Moon

Sigilization

Spare came to prominence with his word sigil for Moon. He questioned the medieval practise of using sigils to evoke entities, arguing that such supernatural beings were simply complexes in the unconcious and could be actively created through the process of 'sigilization'.

Spare's method dispensed with pre-existing esoterica and external beliefs. Sigils were no longer for controlling tradtitional demons and angels, but controlling forces in the unconcious psyche of the individual magician. Sigilisation became the core element of Chaos Magick.

THOUGHT SIGILS

Power
Word Sigil

Statement Sigils

Chaos Magick

Chaos Magick is a contemporary magical practise initially developed in England by Peter J. Carroll during the 1970s and 80s. It draws heavily from the occult philosophies of Austin Osman Spare, whose works are considered foundational reading for Chaos magicians. His technique known as 'sigilization' became the core element of Chaos Magick and has developed into a popular element of western occultism.

Spare died in the 1950s, long before Chaos Magick was thought of. He did not conceive of Chaos Magick but many of his magical beliefs were incorporated into Chaos Magick theory which is about using ideas and practises that are helpful to the magician at the moment, even if they contradict the ideas and practises used previously.

Generally, Chaos Maigick is much less complex than ceremonial magic which depends on specific beliefs and old occult teachings about how the Universe operates, how things relate to each other and how to approach various powers.

Ceremonial magic often refers to authoritative voices from antiquity, such as passages from the Bible, cabalistic teachings or the wisdom of the ancients. None of that matters in Chaos Magick, tapping into magic is personal, willful and most of all psychological.

Spare's spiritual legacy was largely maintained by his friend, the Thelemite author Kenneth Grant. In the later part of the 20th century, Grants belief regarding sigilization provided a key influence on the Chaos Magick movement and the cults of Zos Kia Cultus, Iluminates of Thanatos, Thee Temple ov Psychick Youth and the Church of the Sub-genius.

Chaos magicians have expanded on the basic sigilization technique, inventing new uses for sigils outside of cermony.

The term 'hypersigil' was coined by Grant Morrison who used it to refer to an extended work of art with magical meaning and will power. A traditional sigil is turned into a hypersigil by becoming an extended artistic activity that can take the form of a poem, story, song or dance.

Gordon White developed the technique of 'shoaling' which involves launching a group of sigils for a set of related aims. Instead of sigilizing for 'money', sigilization for a pay rise, new business clients, promotion or a chance win, etc. All of which help 'shift' the probability towards the overall aim.

White also developed the technique of 'robofish' which consists of including a sigil for something that the Chaos magician knows will definitely happen, to 'lead' the rest of the shoal.

Created by the DKMU, the LS or Linking Sigil is an even more recent innovation, used to transfer energy from one place to another. The ELLIS linking sigil is the most famous variant.

In Chaos Magick, sigil, servitor, egregore and godhead form what is called Fluid Continuism. Beginning with a 'dumb' sigil representing something but doesn't actually think. When the dumb sigil has been charged long enough, it can turn into a servitor, which is either completely stupid but capable of doing complex tasks, all the way up to being able to think on its own and deduce things in its operation.

Within Chaos Magick, a servitor is a psychological complex, deliberately created by the magician for a specific purpose that appears to operate autonomously from the magicians consciousness, as if it were an independent, existing being.

When the servitor gets really big, when it becomes more than one person to handle, it becomes an egregore. An egregore is a concept representing a distinct non physical entity that arises from a collective group of people.

At this point it is capable of making some of its own demands, guiding its own work and in general taking on a life of its own. Grant Morrison has argued that modern corporate logos are a form of sigil, a condensation, a compressed symbolic summing up of the word of desire which the corporation intends to represent. Their ever presence in visual life makes corporate logos a form of viral sigil, infecting the mind and polluting the environment.

If an egregore continues to grow it becomes a godhead, something that has grown so strong that the people involved with it take up a subservient relationship, often worshiping it, or appealing to it for help, like the Christian cross.

MacDonalds   Dollar

Hammer and Sickle   Peace

Sigil, Servitor, Ergegore, Godhead

SIGILS

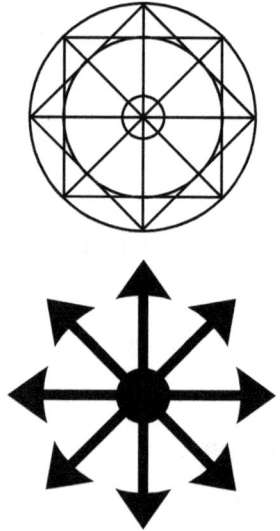

Chaos Star

A servitor constructed from eight arrow headed spokes, the Chaos Star represents the notion of infinate possibilities. It originated in the literary work of science-fantasy author Michael Moorcock's 'The Eternal Changes' of the 1960s.

Since then it has been assimilated into the modern occult tradition, adopted as the emblem of Chaos Magick in the 1970s by Neo Shamanists and by various role playing games.

THOUGHT SIGILS

Illuminates of Thanatos

Chaos Sphere

Chaos Star Variants

Sigil Shoal

CHOSMGIK

Success

"have a nice day"
H V N C D Y

"I will get what I want"
Grant Morrison

Graphic Variation

A quick web search for Chaos Magick sigils will reveal a distinct amount of personal artistic styles created by amateur and serious sigilists alike.

IDESRWOLDPAC
(I desire world peace)

Typographic Sigil
A word or statement sigil is drawn on paper then recreated using DTP software, where the type can be manipulated to create a typographic variant.

Seal of Beelzebub

From the 2007 grimoire of ceremonial magic titled Legion 49 by Barry William Hale. This post-modern seal shows the sigil of Beelzebub inside the Triangle of Arte, surrounded by some of the sigils of his 49 servitors.

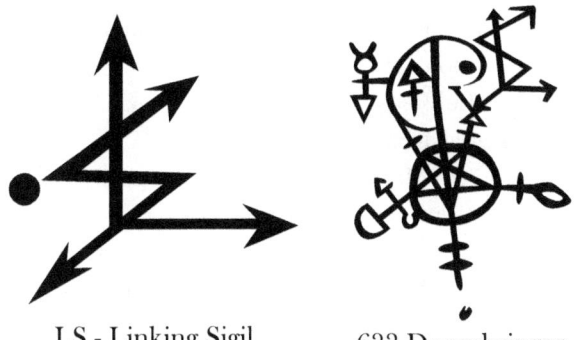

LS - Linking Sigil   633 Doombringer

DKMU

The DKMU began as an autonomous group of artists and occultists that originated from two groups, the Domus Kaotice and the Marauder Underground. A mixture of Chaos Magick, Shamanism, Voodoo and ceremonial magic, the DKMU utilize guerilla tactics to spread the Assault on Reality.

The Assault on Reality and the LS or Linking Sigil created in 2004 are their predominant works, supplemented by a series of inhouse godforms published in the Liber Sigillum in 2016.

This grimoire reveals the magic ceremonies and invocations used to summon the DKMU egregores and godheads.

Further Reading

Testament of Solomon - 8th c. Arabic

Book of Honorus - 13th c. French

Book of Abramelin - 1400 German

Magical Treatise of Solomon - 14th c. Greek

Biblioteca Magna Rabbinica - Bartolozzi 15th c.

Pseudomaonarchia Daemonum - Weyer 1577

Da Philosophica Occulta - H. C. Agrippa 1531-1533

(Greater) Keys of Solomon - 15th c. Italian

Sefer Raziel - 15th century Jewish

Black Venus - Dr John Dee 16th c.

First Five Books of the Mysteries - Dr John Dee 16th c.

Liber Loagath - Dr John Dee 16th c.

Lesser Keys of Solomon - 1750s Italian

Sefer Zohar - 13th century Jewish

Black Pullet - 18th century French

Grimoirium Verum - 18th c. Swiss

The Magus - Francis Barrett 1801

The Book of the Goetia of Solomon the King - MacGregore Mathers / Crowley 1904

777 and other Cabalistic Mysteries - A. Crowley 1909

Book of Pleasure - Austin Osman Spare 1913

Legion 49 - Barry William Hale 2007

Liber Sigillum - Frater E. S. 2012

esotericarchives.com

sacredtexts.com

gromioresite.wordpress.com

bookofsymbols.wordpress.com

occult-study.org

symbolikon.com

symboldictionary.net

spellsandmagic.org

studies-vartejaru.blogspot.com

paranormalknowledge.com

visualmelt.com

scienceandsigils.wordpress.com

torrdaniel.com

archive.org

lewlelyn.com

digitalambler.com

dkmu.org

www.ingramcontent.com/pod-product-compliance
Lightning Source LLC
Chambersburg PA
CBHW070639050426
42451CB00008B/229

Sigils are symbolic icons designed for a specific magical purpose. The Christian church acknowledged the sigil as an occult device originating in astrology.

Traditionally, sigils are line diagrams representing the signature of a planetary, elemental, angelic or demonic spirit used in the ceremonial magic developed during the Middle Ages and the Renaissance.

Such sigils were derived from the spirits themselves or divined by magicians using various numerological techniques.

In modern times, Chaos magicians employ sigils as Monograms of Thought, psychological symbols of intent and desire, created by the conjuror in their personal quest of mystical exploration.